FINDING
MY GOD

AN EIGHTY-YEAR JOURNEY

Robert D. Goldbach

Finding My God
An Eighty-Year Journey

2015: First Edition
Subject Index:
Goldbach, Robert D.
Title: Finding My God: An Eighty-Year Journey
1.   Finding God 2. Finding My God 3. Big Bang 4. Infinite God 5. Eternal God 6. Pervasive God
ISBN-13:
978-0-9910985-2-1

Front Cover Photograph Courtesy Paul Aranha, Nassau Bahamas
islandairman@gmail.com

WRITTEN IN MEMORY
OF
DR. R. MAURICE BOYD
1932–2009

Born in Belfast, Ireland, Dr. Boyd was a preacher, author, and lecturer of international renown, and created a radio ministry that engaged listeners throughout the New York area. His service to God spanned almost sixty-five years. He served as Senior Minister of Metropolitan Church in London, Ontario; Fifth Avenue Presbyterian Church in New York City; and ultimately, The City Church, New York, an independent, interdenominational organization founded in 1993 to advance his ministry.

Maurice was both friend and pastor for twenty-five years.

Robert D. Goldbach
August 2015

Contents

Foreword

Since entering Webb Institute six decades ago, Robert Goldbach and I have had a series of conversations and correspondence growing ever more profound. I suspect that all believers (and probably non-believers) are theologians. The development of Rob's book over the past several years supports my hunch.

Our undergraduate study introduced us deeply to technology and science, but was also an experience of character formation, critical analysis and systemic perception. Rob's theology and my own are deeply rooted there. We have a great appreciation for that which we call objective, what can be weighed, measured, worked through hypothesis and practice, and then yield accepted theory. We also work with subjective spiritual experiences, questions, and reflection, and are open to their observable effects. Out of this, each of us has come to a place of acceptance of God's will or plan, and trust in God, prayer as dialogue, and a conviction that God indeed has influence in us and all creation.

Great breadth and variation of understanding typify all faiths as humans struggle to state the inexpressible and describe the incomprehensible. I am struck by Rob's coming to call the divine "My God." It reminds me of Jesus' calling God his Father (and hence our Father). Jesus' Aramaic word for Father, "Abba," implies the intimacy and trust of a little one in a good and loving dad – or mom. *Finding My God* is an intimate book. We are privileged that Rob opens himself to us as he has opened himself to God.

I am among those who apply Biblical Criticism, archeology, and historical context to the understanding and application of the Holy Bible. As others have said, this means taking the Bible seriously, although not literally. Reading Rob's work has also helped crystallize in my mind that we need to treat the historic dogmas and doctrines of the church critically, culturally and historically. Thank you, Rob.

Readers, you may be more wedded to traditional statements of faith than Rob's conclusions. I hope you will enter into dialogue in your own minds with Rob. I invite you to apply your critical thinking to what he has written just as he has considered critically what others have stated. It is a fruitful exercise. I have grown by engaging Rob's spirituality and understanding. He offers his conclusions with the same humility he has found in God, and entrusts them to us as he entrusts himself to God.

I offer a suggestion for reading and engaging with *Finding My God*. Rob writes about many topics and themes. He applies his observations and conclusions from nature and spirituality to each in turn. Rather than only reading *Finding My God* from cover to cover, I believe we will find it profitable to read and reflect on it chapter by chapter, perhaps a section per week. Taking time to reflect on such themes aids spiritual growth. Again, thank you, Rob, for your engaging invitation.

Charlie Grover
(The Rev. Charles L. Grover, III)

Chapter One

Beginning An Eighty-Year Journey

*It took almost eighty years, but I finally found a God I hope to know for all of eternity, a God I call **"my God."***

Until the end was in sight, I was content for my journey to remain an untold story. I'm not one to talk about myself and a book coach added further discouragement by advising me that no one is interested in what a non-cleric has to say about religion anyway. I certainly have views on various religions, but the only one I want to share is any religion that brings people closer to God, is a good thing.

As an engineer, I arrive at my faith through a more rigorous and analytical approach, while my wife Dottie relies upon her superb intuitive and caring nature to find the right side of every situation. Faith that results from lifelong exposure to religion is personal and unique to each of us.

Somehow we usually manage to come out at the same place on faith, but then we fell in love almost sixty five years ago and have shared most of what life brought our way since then. We have a large extended family spanning four generations and we care greatly for all of them. Not too long ago, I decided to write something that might help them, and those who come after them, know us when we are gone. While Dottie would no doubt express herself quite differently, I have endeavored to include in this work nothing with which she might find disagreement.

As work progressed, I learned a lot about what I really believed by trying to find words to explain it in a way cynics might consider credible. I recommend the exercise for anyone who considers him or herself to be a Believer. Saying one believes in God is much easier than presenting a persuasive and pragmatic case for why one has placed faith in God, especially when one finds conflicting interpretations of ancient scripture that are difficult to rationalize with the world we know exists. Theologians, philosophers and educators are far more qualified than I to explain how great faith can overcome those conflicts. Much of their excellent work can be found in modern literature and I would not presume to add to it.

This final work relies upon factual information from trusted sources, including scripture, and draws from that information conclusions that minimize reliance on blind faith. If parts of it are helpful to persons outside our family, I would be more than pleased.

My brothers and I lived our early years before, during and after World War II in a New Jersey town having the curious of Scotch Plains. Our parents encouraged church attendance after we entered first grade, and that normally involved walking one mile each way. Gasoline was rationed for the war and our father needed all of it for commuting to his job in defense of our country.

They rarely attended church themselves, but both parents had deeply rooted standards for right and wrong that they passed on to their children. We were lovingly raised by a mother who simply trusted God would look after all of us and a father who had been turned against organized religion by an experience involving one of its practitioners.

After his death in 1991, I pieced together details he shared with different family members and information then coming to public attention. I concluded that he witnessed abuse by a cleric and did not wish to speak about it. Deep down in my estimation he still placed his faith in God and he certainly believed in doing good things. He was the kindest, most considerate man I have ever known.

My identical twin Rich and I were inseparable, and attended Sunday school at the Baptist Church, which was the largest in our small town at the time. All Saints was the competing Episcopal Church on the other side of town. It was struggling at the time and kept its doors open only by the selfless efforts of its Minister. Dr. William Basil, and its organist/choir director Torrence Kynes, who everyone addressed as Mr. Kynes.

All Saints had neither sufficient members nor funds for an adult choir, so Mr. Kynes assembled a dozen or so musically inclined pre-teen boys of various religious persuasions to serve as choristers for Sunday worship. My brother Rich and I started our first job in life, at the age of nine, singing in that choir on Sunday and attending two weekday evening practices in exchange for a salary of seventy five cents per week.

By that time we had acquired WWII vintage bicycles that were vitally needed to leave church school at 10:45 and be fully bedecked in our vestments in time for the 11:00 processional at All Saints. This was not an easy task considering the vestments included a black full length gown with many buttons down the front, a white coverlet over the torso, a stiff white collar kept closed by a brass collar button, and a long black ribbon around the neck that each chorister fashioned into his own version of a bow tie.

Despite our comparatively poor singing ability, for the three years we sang in his choir Mr. Kynes seemed to like Rich and me, and drove us to and from choir practice held in the evening after his work day was finished. He also gave us an undeserved twenty five cent increase in pay after two years. Most of the boys were taller than him, but he had great dignity and always wore a white dress shirt, tie, and matching suit of clothes including vest. He loved being a choir director and organist, never missed a practice or service and kept a restless group of choristers under control during Sunday worship by staring them down across the chancel from behind his organ.

One of his favorite hymns was *All in an April Evening*. It describes the Passion of Jesus allegorically and tore at my heart every time we sang it.

*All in an April evening
April airs were abroad;
The sheep with their little lambs
Passed me by on the road.*

*The lambs were weary, and crying
With a weak human cry;
I thought on the Lamb of God
Going meekly to die…*
                          - Hugh S. Roberton

Our family moved away after three years and I never saw him again. We exchanged notes on Christmas cards for fifteen years until I received a letter from his daughter that he had died. This work discusses *my God's* spiritual qualities epitomized in Jesus Christ and found in varying degrees in His followers. Torrence Kynes opened my eyes to those qualities, and more than anyone else inspired me at the beginning of my journey.

Chapter Two

Seeking God

My brothers and I grew up in modest circumstances during a time when all Americans were greatly affected by war with the Germans and Japanese and threat of war with Russia.

The times were challenging, but I think it was a good start, and as a young boy I was content to accept God purely on what I now recognize as blind faith. As I matured, I endeavored to use some of the intelligence, education, wisdom and experience I acquired to reinforce my belief in His existence, discern His nature, and eventually try to please Him. I also grew in recognition and understanding of the many who, for various reasons, deny God.

Along the way, I learned that there is much more to faith than attending church on Sunday and returning to ordinary life during the rest of the week. I loved celebrating the coming of Christ during Advent and Christmas, and reliving his life and resurrection during Lent and Easter week. Over a lifetime of almost eighty years, these important events gradually diminished in value as they became overwhelmed by commercial activity that distracted from their spiritual significance. In time I began to look beyond the events to seek a deeper understanding of Jesus Christ and the God He represented.

Not all of humanity may accept the *existence* of God, but I believe every human has a degree of ability to consider *evidence* of an existent God when and if it is brought to their attention. Some may nevertheless choose to deny that evidence. In my case, reaching out to Him opened the door to His existence and added meaning and guidance to my life. If we reach out to God, He stands ready to communicate His unique expectations for each of us and help us carry out His plans.

We are inclined to think life is all about us. Much of it probably is, but in a larger sense, I think there are unique contributions each of us can make in furthering God's plan for our world. Faith, in my estimation, involves acceptance that an incomprehensible God exists and has such a plan. Every part of His plan is good, and if we reach out to Him, we will learn how we can help advance it.

Worship, the the act of demonstrating faith in such a God, may be an important part of the process, but more than that is surely needed if God's plan is to be realized.

People much more knowledgeable than I have found all the answers they need from scripture. I think I have been far from alone in seeking pragmatic fact-based answers that go beyond individual interpretations of scripture that was written in a time when most of the world was illiterate and scientific knowledge was non-existent. Scripture tells of events when God communicated with individuals or groups of individuals. My desire has been to communicate directly with God, if possible, and factor His perceived responses into what I believed to be true from scripture and life experience.

Toward the end, I began to feel comfortable with answers I found to some long held questions on faith and God's existence. Is He external to us or alive in us or both? If Heaven exists, what is its nature and who should expect to be a part of it? Are there eternal consequences to how we conduct our lives? Is it ever too late to turn to Him? I suspect these kinds of questions confront many of us but most septuagenarians have plenty of time to think about it while we are running out of time.

The faith that I carry to life's end is the result of efforts to discern truth through open-minded investigation of scripture, a level of acquired technical knowledge and scientific fact, as well as persuasive Judeo-Christian wisdom from individuals I respect. I endeavoured to reach out to Him for guidance.

Thanks to those efforts I now believe *my God* is nowhere to be found in the adversity that affects all of humanity in various ways and instead shares that adversity with us. A world of adversity existed long before we were born and will surely exist after we die. Yet with His guidance, each of us can help overcome adversity even if along the way we occasionally contribute to it. *My God* wants us to understand that the world was imperfect when we were born into it and with His presence in our lives we can contribute to making it better.

"I have come to believe that the mind of God can influence humanity even when it does not invite Him in."

In this work, I draw a somewhat fuzzy line between Jesus the man, and Jesus Christ the man totally inhabited by God as an example to all who follow Him. I suspect such a line existed and do not believe that precludes me from claiming to be a Christian. In fact, it helps me appreciate how so many people in today's world can honestly consider themselves to be Christians. The line is simply drawn in a different place for each of us.

I am persuaded that God was revealed to the world by Jesus and is the God of Abraham and Moses as well. The defining difference, in my view, is that *my God* acted through Jesus, while Abraham and Moses reached out to Him. They communicated directly with Him and became His advocates and servants. Followers of Jesus Christ, in my opinion, accept that a spiritual God is part of their very existence, cooperate with His will made known to them, and welcome Him to do His work through them. On the other hand, non-Christians act in accordance with direction they perceive as coming from God. A distinction without a difference for some, perhaps, but not for me.

Much of my journey has been about trying to understand in a manner I consider credible how an existent God having no physicality might accomplish His will in a physical world. I have had no "encounter" with God and I think rather than accomplishing His will through encounters, He instead does it by getting into the minds of those possessing both brainpower and physicality, whether they believe in Him or not. What we do as individuals when that happens, is of course the big question, but it stands to reason that if we have opened the door to His existence we are more likely to discern and accomplish God's will as He has communicated it to us.

I'm neither a scholar of the Holy Bible or the Qur'an, but if He is to be found in both books, neither contains all the answers and there is more to be learned about God and His will. Most of the information that these two books contain may be timeless, but they were written between fourteen hundred and thirty four hundred years ago, when most of the world was illiterate, scientific knowledge was nonexistent, and no one had the slightest clue that the Universe was fourteen billion years old, and life on earth had been evolving for three billion years prior.

Documentation of enlightenment was in the hands of a small

minority of erudite persons that did not include Abraham, Jesus or Muhammad. Few today understand the circumstances or language that existed when these texts were written, and history would indicate that spiritual leaders who interpret and indeed translate either book, are not strangers to human imperfection. The well-intentioned can misunderstand or misstate God's intended message, and the poorly intentioned are fully capable of deliberate distortion for personal advantage.

Religion as a Path that Leads to Truth

I have lived in almost twenty different locations and been associated with eight different Protestant denominations, each of whom had specific enumerated beliefs not particularly enforced among its adherents. I am less familiar with Roman Catholicism, but my impression is that the faith of adherents is measured by willingness to observe established dogma. I was never able to accept all the professed beliefs of the Protestant denomination to which I then belonged. I did not consider it necessary or even productive to speak out, enjoying instead the opportunity to be a part of the fine work that each was accomplishing.

Each association brought me closer to understanding and wanting to worship *my God* and Jesus Christ. I have been influenced by the preaching of several fine ministers, but I think my search for truth began in earnest some thirty years ago when I first encountered Dr. R. Maurice Boyd, to whom this book is dedicated. Maurice died in 2009 and I miss him greatly, even though Dottie and I feel at home in our current Nassau Bahamas church.

We regularly visit the Chautauqua Institution in western New York State. Maurice was honored twice by being invited to preach the weekly series of five morning sermons at its 5000 seat open air amphitheater. Founded in 1874, Chautauqua is dedicated to the exploration of the best in human values and the enrichment of life through a nine week summer program of civil discourse that explores the important religious, social and political issues of our times.

In 2014 we attended five afternoon lectures at Chautauqua by mid-octogenarian John Shelby Spong, all delivered to record breaking audiences, and God willing, we will attend five more in 2016. Long retired from active ministry, Spong served as bishop of the Episcopal Diocese of Newark, New Jersey for 24 years; pioneered the movement starting thirty years ago to welcome gays and lesbians into the Christian Church; has written several best-selling books on faith; and continues to serve God today as an amazing biblical scholar, analyst, and teacher delivering 200 lectures per year. He is a committed Christian who has spent a lifetime studying the Bible and whose life has been shaped by it.

Thanks to Bishop Spong, Dottie and I now understand we are far from alone in our inability to accept certain professed beliefs of various Protestant denominations and this work has been influenced by his perceptive writing. "Once we begin to see the Passion narrative not as history but as liturgy that was created to interpret the meaning of Jesus ... those who long ago ceased to accept the Bible and its stories as literal truth, and who have dismissed the whole Christian story as a fantasy, begin suddenly to see some new possibilities." I commend the writing of Bishop Spong to all who, like me, struggle to accept the literal truth of much that is found in the Bible.

I would never presume to interpret the Bible for others; that is better done by persons far more qualified than I. *Finding My God* instead tells the story of my own imperfect search for truth during a wonderful life of my own choosing. Maurice Boyd often discussed the difference between an opinion having narrow basis and a point of view based on the best information available. This work represents my point of view based upon answers coming my way from life experiences and sources I respect, including some that came in the quiet of the night. By sharing it, I hope to reinforce the faith of some who are already believers and provide pragmatic encouragement to others who question or even deny God's very existence.

Chapter Three

Finding My God

I found an all-knowing, eternal and infinite spiritual reality pervading all that has been, all that is, and all that will be. The Bible was enormously helpful but in order to best understand His reality I needed also to open the door to God and seek further truth that only became known after the Bible was written.

In Revelation 3, John writes, "Behold, I stand at the door and knock. If anyone hears my voice and opens the door I will come in to him." Jesus helped explain what that meant when he told Nicodemus that flesh gives birth to flesh and spirit gives birth to spirit.

In order to be one with an unseen God what seems clear to me from this Scripture is that during physical life we need to find our way into (be born into) a spiritual world that co-exists with our physical world but is separate and distinct from it. Being "born again" is surely a figure of speech and does not mean that we need to be born physically two times. Nor does it mean that there is a distinction between so-called "born again" Christians and all other Christians. I think one needs to seek and find the spiritual God who was revealed in Jesus Christ in order to consider him or herself a Christian. In this work, I call Him "*my God*" and it was through Jesus Christ that I found Him.

I see a purely spiritual God who has an ultimate intention, can communicate with all who listen and acts only through those who acknowledge Him and invite Him to accomplish His will through them. *My God* knows what He wants to accomplish and how and when it can best be accomplished by those who open the door to Him. He knows when He needs humanity to act and when humanity should be free to enjoy lives of their own choosing. He is fully aware that others who do not reach out to Him are pursuing their own agenda and the instruction He communicates takes that reality into account.

When *my God* acts, He does so by communicating to and through humanity in a manner and on a schedule that He thinks will accomplish the greatest good. His communications could be revealed through experiences in life or voices or writings of persons we respect and they could also come directly from Him in the silence of the night. As I describe in this work our minds must be open to His responses and it is still up to us to determine what action we take when we receive them. No approach by me has ever gone unanswered, but His responses were not always what I expected or even hoped for, and they certainly came on His schedule and not mine. When they came, they were unmistakable as coming from Him and it was up to me whether to be receptive to them. I didn't always pass that test.

Understanding *My God*

I don't think we need to be concerned with how well we articulate ourselves when we speak to Him; my infinite and pervasive God will know what is in our minds and has been waiting for us to open the door and welcome Him into our lives. We should not be surprised if He occasionally provides answers that go beyond what we thought we were asking.

Christians and Jews are taught that God created the heavens and the earth, and science has already proven that everything in our physical Universe, including time and space, were created by the Big Bang. For both of those things to be true my purely spiritual God would have needed to be instrumental in causing the Big Bang. Many believe that God willed the universe into being before time, space and physicality even existed. Stephen Hawking clearly disagrees.

From my perspective, this question does not need to be resolved in order to still believe that *my God* is spiritually alive in our Universe and has been since the beginning of time. If as I believe, He exists only as a spiritual reality, His domain is arguably infinite, eternal, and all-pervasive. Stephen Hawking may well be right that our Universe is one of many, but why should we think only in terms of our Universe when we speak of God? And why should we rule out that He was simply as present at the instant of the Big Bang as He is now?

Many deny God's existence merely because they cannot comprehend it, but such an enormous presence is beyond anyone's comprehension and can only be accepted through faith. There have been countless times when His presence has been felt and evidence of His work has been witnessed but there is no historical record, biblical or otherwise, of anyone claiming to have seen a physical God. Many are inclined to personalize Him in an effort to comprehend the incomprehensible but personalizing Him can lead to assumptions that He has physicality and exists for us, rather than us for Him.

For Believers and non-believers alike, it would appear only

natural to think of Him in quantifiable terms. If a single mono-theistic God indeed exists He is surely infinite and eternal, making no mistakes, inhabiting His entire domain including our Universe and infinitely superior in every way to anything else that inhabits it. Without His help, that makes *my God* incomprehensible to mere mortals, particularly those who refuse even to consider efforts on His part to reveal His nature. In my life I have found reason to believe that *my God* stands ready to reveal much about Himself, including His wishes for humanity, in a manner comprehensible to any who seek Him.

I am a Christian because I have been persuaded that even though God may have communicated His wishes to and through a great number of persons before the coming of Jesus, including Abraham and Moses, it was through Jesus Christ that *my God's* fundamental nature was first revealed. To put it another way, *my God* became one with humanity for the first time through the ministry of Jesus Christ and His light shone through Jesus. The more humankind chooses to seek Him, respect the wishes He communicates, and emulate His spiritual qualities revealed in Jesus Christ the more reason there is to expect *my God* will be pleased and much good will result. If worship is the act of imparting great value and reverence to those who do only good, then *my God* and Jesus Christ are both to be worshiped.

According to scripture, Jesus was compassionate, wise, humble, just, merciful, forgiving, understanding, slow to anger, and free-willed. Intelligent life also possesses these qualities; uniquely, individually and to varied degrees. These are the spiritual qualities of the God I worship, and in Jesus Christ they were perfect, making him the epitome of compassion, wisdom, humility, justice, mercy, forgiveness, understanding, patience and free will.

I choose the quality of "compassion" rather than "love" because compassion is a feeling of deep sympathy and sorrow for those stricken by misfortune accompanied by a strong desire to alleviate suffering. Compassion is the highest form of love, comparable to the love of a mother for a child carried in her womb.

Countless fine persons over the course of history have questioned the existence of any god but have nevertheless led good lives, at least based upon the qualities of compassion, wisdom, humility, justice, mercy, forgiveness, understanding and patience that were revealed in Jesus.

Like my father, many really believed in a God and simply found organized religions wanting, but there is no denying the great number of atheists who possess fine human qualities and yet believe they, and not God, determine what is good. My answer to those atheists who intend no harm is that there is plenty of room for them in *my God's* world. He has compassion for them, even though His love may not be reciprocated.

My God pervades all that has been created and relies upon humankind to invite His guidance in carrying out His will. Living a good life may ensure that no harm is done, and emulating Jesus' spiritual qualities is a good start, but in order for humanity to accomplish His will I believe He needs individual endeavor guided by direct and personal communication with Him. Much more might have been accomplished by now if those who questioned God's existence had instead reached out to Him, but my infinite and patient God has plenty of time.

My God is not a micromanager of a living earthly presence endowed with free will. Instead, He provides guidance to those who choose to reach out to Him. It is not in His nature to exact earthly punishment on those who displease Him. Any perceived punishment is the result of life's free willed activity, including one's own, but occasionally continuing natural activity resulting from the Big Bang plays a part.

A Work in Progress

It has been helpful for me to think of *my God's* intention for our world as being a work in progress. Modern humanity is central to its success but has only been around for some 200,000 years. Humans have a way of producing new life and dying long before they achieve an age of one hundred years so continuity is an issue. Every new life has the potential to serve *my God,* but they need first to find Him and enlist His assistance in how they can best make a contribution. Many and possibly most fail to make the effort, but *my God* can advance His intention without them, and sometimes in spite of them, by working through those who are committed to serving Him.

Such a god as *my God* is surely more focused on what He wants to accomplish in the future than what failed to be accomplished in the past because of inadequacies of humanity. He knows very well the challenges that come with relying on a humanity that is individually and collectively imperfect and expecting them to reach out to Him first. This focus on the future, in my opinion, explains both His willingness to be forgiving and His need for those committed to Him to reach out to the uncommitted. He needs all the help He can get.

Christians are told to "follow Christ," but many who accept God do not accept that Jesus Christ and God are one and the same. *My God* inhabited Jesus in order to reveal His nature to humanity and accomplish His will through Jesus and those who choose to emulate him. I haven't found many who think of the relationship between God and Jesus Christ in quite that way.

Knowledgeable biblical scholars, including Bishop Spong,

believe that many of Jesus' words and deeds described in the Gospels of Matthew, Mark, Luke and John, all written by Jews, reflected Jewish mysticism of the first century CE when the emphasis of Christianity was on convincing Jews that Jesus was their Messiah.

My faith does not rely on any of the precise words, acts, or miracles attributable to Jesus, nor does it rely on a belief that God and Jesus Christ are one and the same. I am content with a physical Jesus totally inhabited by my spiritual God who is ready to inhabit all who invite Him in. Some would deny my right to call myself a Christian for that reason alone, but I don't see it that way. I think *my God* decided it was time to accomplish His will by inhabiting humanity rather than relying only upon third-party communication of His will and hoping for the best. Jesus may have been inhabited to the greatest extent, but many followers of Jesus Christ have welcomed *my God* into their lives, and our world is better for it.

Nor do I think only Christians help carry out His will in our world. My God communicates His will to countless non-Christians, and much is accomplished when they in turn carry out or communicate His will. If they understood and accepted His nature, revealed in Jesus Christ, and if they welcomed His spirit into their very being, they could perhaps do so more effectively.

I share the imperfection of humankind and make no claim to more perfect knowledge than anyone else. I have spent much time and effort trying to come to an understanding of a God I could relate to and understand. I approach the end of my days content that I have done my best to find Him.

Chapter Four

The Big Bang

Faith in my God *does not require belief that He had a hand in either the creation of the Universe or the origin of humankind.*

I think it is a mistake to be overly concerned with conflicts between belief in God and scientific knowledge, at least until the time comes that science is able to rigorously refute His existence. Scientists are obviously in the business of following the physical evidence to determine what is demonstrably true and not what might be true, if only they had confidence in a few more facts. Until an infinite, eternal, and purely spiritual God is scientifically proven to exist "beyond a reasonable doubt," I am content to accept my God based on analysis of the "preponderance of evidence." I have not found a preponderance of evidence to indicate that *my God* created a universe and world "just for us." In *The Grand Design* Stephen Hawking, the world's foremost astrophysicist, concludes that the hand of God was not necessary for the Big Bang to occur.

Except for a few of us fortunate ones, most who enter this world leave it without having enjoyed much or any of it while they were here. No god that I could ever worship would wish a legacy of suffering and deprivation for the many in order to benefit the few *as an end result.* Far more likely, in my estimation, is for Him to selectively make use of all life, including humanity, to carry out an ultimate intention that includes an eventual end to suffering and deprivation.

Great comfort can be taken from this alternative. Since the Big Bang our physical Universe has been evolving through various cosmological events like supernovas and black hole formations, and our earth has been evolving through cataclysmic floods, earthquakes, volcanic eruptions, hurricanes, tsunamis and the like. It is arguably far more likely that such events are continuing effects of the Big Bang explosion, rather than angry and vengeful acts taken at points in time by a God worthy of worship.

An infinite, eternal, pervasive, and purely spiritual God who already existed at the time of the Big Bang might well know all that is in the Universe and all that it will be at any point in time, but have no physical ability to micromanage its development. Once life was introduced into our world, such a God would no doubt understand how it could evolve on its own into myriad variations all able to successfully inhabit the environment He knew would exist. He would also understand how life might someday be used by Him to accomplish the physical change He needed to implement His will for our world.

"I believe in a God that is working with what He has. He probably didn't create the Big Bang. He desires for us to carry out His will."

The Grand Design approach would seem to place humankind at the very center of things and make God's work all about us. Many people believe this and Jesus reportedly alluded to it, but it leads to an expectation of a God who responds to our own perceived needs and wishes; in other words, a God who is our servant. If there is indeed a God, the reverse must be true: that we are not only His servants intended to carry out His will, but probably His primary servants. One would think God would choose the best and brightest to be His primary servants.

An infinite God surely has foreknowledge not only of cataclysmic events resulting from the Big Bang, but also the ability of humankind to endure them. Why then should such events be intended to punish us for bad acts? They are likely not bad, but simply challenging. Humanity is capable of confronting all challenges, even at the cost of some sacrifice. We please Him by accepting whatever challenges come our way and confronting them to the best of our ability.

A Universal Matter

Modern science has proved conclusively that everything associated with our Universe originated with the Big Bang. When I attended engineering school many years ago we were taught to think in terms of energy and matter being the basic building blocks of the Universe. We learned how to develop Einstein's formula relating energy to mass and the speed of light and were taught that his theory of relativity demonstrated that nothing in the Universe can exceed the speed of light of 186,000 miles per second.

Anyone studying physics at the time I was studying engineering knew things were far more complex than that and in any event the world of physics has progressed at lightning speed since then. The Universe is far more complicated than I had been led to believe many years ago and no one can explain it better than Stephen Hawking. Much of what he writes may be beyond me but some is not and I find it very helpful.

Science knows that time and space were created by the Big Bang but admits that it fully understands less than 5% of what they think is needed for the Universe to make sense. They apparently have insufficient scientific proof about the other 96% or so but widely accepted progress has been made. So-called anti-matter, said to comprise 23%, and dark energy, said to comprise 73%, are thought to make up the difference, even though they are not yet fully understood. The thinking seems to be based upon a presumption that the content of the Universe can neither be added to nor destroyed. Taking pluses and minuses into account, the sum of everything in the physical Universe must be zero or close to zero, as it was at the time of the Big Bang.

The Big Bang would therefore have created an incomprehensibly enormous collection of pluses and minuses from virtually nothing and the obvious question is whether the Big Bang just happened or was made to happen. Judging from *The Grand Design* Stephen Hawking is of the opinion that action by a God was not needed for the Big Bang to happen and his opinion may well become established scientific fact in the near future. When that happens it will clearly bring into question the traditional belief of Judeo Christians in a God who is creator of all that exists in our physical Universe. Hawking seems to think it disproves any need for God.

Hawking's remarkable efforts have not, in my opinion, disproven the existence of a purely spiritual God responsible for creating *all that is good* in our Universe, and accomplishing it over time following the Big Bang. I endeavor in this work to explain why I believe such a God exists and is worthy of worship.

My infinite and purely spiritual God existed when time itself was created by the Big Bang, and His pervasive spirit inhabits His entire domain, including all of humanity. I am persuaded that His spiritual qualities were revealed through the life of Jesus, that He has an ability to communicate with anyone who will listen, that

His spirit does its will through those who welcome Him into their lives, that He is content with imperfection in humanity, and that the best way to know Him is through Jesus Christ. I explore in this work how my spiritual God overcomes His absence of physicality with the help of those who seek Him, listen to Him and act upon His guidance.

I think there is plenty of reason to believe our physical world is still evolving and that a purely spiritual God needs a living physical presence to help Him realize His intended outcome. Creation is an ongoing process and humanity plays an important role.

Whether or not God created our physical Universe is less important to me than whether He has been present in our Universe since its very beginning. My belief in such a presence is based upon a bedrock conviction that there is a single eternal purpose for life as we know it, particularly human life.

Any plan of an existent God for our Universe and the reasoning for it are surely beyond human comprehension, but we will no doubt please Him by accepting that He exists and has a plan. We can also reach out to Him regarding how we might further His plan and live our lives in furtherance of what we perceive He has communicated to us. This is where faith is needed and I have placed my faith in an existent God I call "*my God*".

Chapter Five

My God Reveals Himself to the World

Whether or not He initiated the Big Bang, my infinite and eternal God had a purpose for our world long before it existed.

Perhaps it's the engineer in me, but I have great interest in understanding how a world of uniquely and individually different life forms fits into the accomplishment of that purpose and why He would not simply say "Let it be so." Time and space may exist for us and not for Him, and fourteen billion years may be a blink of an eye for *my God*, but we are clearly a world of life forms that make our own decisions influenced by random physical events and past less than perfect choices either made by us or made for us by others. We do not even trust each other, so why should He entrust us with a meaningful role in implementing His plan? Perhaps He shouldn't trust any of us, but it appears He does in fact place great reliance on those who trust Him.

An eternal spiritual reality that epitomizes humility could very well love everything created after the Big Bang but have no ability to directly intervene physically. He could, however, do so indirectly by spiritual influence, including communicating His will to and through those with intelligence who are able to serve Him. He could do so most effectively in response to an invitation by or on behalf of someone who possesses the needed life experiences and creative, intellectual and physical ability to discern His will and act upon it. I am persuaded that *my God* accomplishes His will when and if invited and has the ability to determine which invitations are worthy of His intervention.

It would seem self-evident that all life is endowed with unique ability to survive, reproduce, adapt to its environment, and exercise free will without any intervention from *my God*, but that doesn't rule out an ultimate purpose for life in our world. *My God* is perfectly capable of accomplishing His will using those who turn to Him.

Human choices matter greatly to *my God's* plan, and He no doubt would like for them to be good ones, but it is His nature to accomplish His will by influencing decisions and not making them for us. Bad choices are still possible, especially when He is not even consulted. *My God* chose humankind to implement His will, but how and when that happens is in the hands of humankind.

Following the Big Bang, I think *my God* needed to let it play out on its own for the better part of fourteen billion years before our world was ready for Him to employ humanity in carrying out His will.

It would not have been productive to reveal Himself when humanity was evolving physically and intellectually from the animal world and had not yet acquired the ability to reason. It also would not have been productive to reveal Himself until there was sufficient intelligence to understand that He existed and respect His enormity and what He stood for. Anatomically modern humans had existed for over 4 million years before humanity acquired the ability to reason, perceived *my God's* presence and began to reach out to Him.

My God chose to start small and in one venue. He needed to build upon a committed community of Believers with strong leadership and thirty-eight hundred years ago He chose the people of Israel to get started on His work with humankind. Sophisticated Egyptian, Indian and Chinese civilizations were around at the time of His revelation to Abraham but He nonetheless "chose" the people of Israel to get started, probably because of their particular combination of intelligence, wisdom, industriousness, patience and perseverance. Most modern-day Jews still possess these characteristics and some consider having been so "chosen" as deserving of a special place in His eyes today. *My God* no doubt loves the Jews and equally loves all that has been created. He may have revealed His *existence* to the Jews but I think He revealed His *nature* through Jesus Christ.

Since that time thirty-eight hundred years ago, *my God* has communicated His will to all who reached out to Him for themselves or others. This includes many who not only reacted to His message as they perceived it but also shared it with others, often with a degree of human imperfection. Christians, Jews and Muslims alike have tried to please Him by acting in accordance with His will as it has been so shared. I think *my God* has unique and personal guidance for everyone who turns to Him and that guidance is most effectively communicated directly and in response to personal petition.

After eighteen hundred years spent preparing the Jews to receive Him, *my God* decided it was time to begin communicating His message through them as well as to them. Upon conscious invitation from Jesus *my God's* spirit inhabited him. Not only did *my God's* revelations come through Jesus, His spiritual qualities became those of Jesus Christ. Those who know Jesus Christ also know much about *my God*.

Until Jesus' ministry *my God* arguably communicated His will for humanity only responsively. With Jesus' ministry he began also to communicate His will through the life of Jesus. In order to do this effectively He needed His spiritual qualities to be reflected in Jesus. With Jesus Christ *my God* became one with humanity and in my judgment has been one with humanity ever since through those who, like Jesus, have welcomed Him to do His will through them. As Paul writes in his second letter to the people of Corinth, God was in Jesus reconciling the world to Himself and through the life of Jesus He was establishing His relationship with humankind.

The physical death of Jesus Christ was no reason to become external to humanity once again. *My God* was with Jesus when he died, and shared with him His agonizing death as described in the Bible. By the death of Jesus Christ his ministry was dramatized for all time. If he had lived a full life and died an ordinary death, history may well not have remembered him.

My God became one with humanity through Jesus Christ, and I think He intends to stay that way. What better way than to continue to be alive through those who believe He was incarnate in Jesus Christ and turn to Him for guidance? *My God* may have started reconciling the world to Himself with the life of Jesus, but the work continued first through Jesus' apostles and finally through those who seek Him out and choose to serve Him. The Gospels certainly confirm that this was Jesus' wish.

Chapter Six

Jesus Christ

My faith relies on a conviction that during his ministry Jesus was totally inhabited by my God.

Christians are taught to believe that God and Jesus Christ are one, and most non-Christians find this very difficult to accept. In my view Jesus, during his ministry on earth, was totally inhabited by my purely spiritual God. By the example of Jesus, all who chose to follow him would know God's nature and invite Him to use them to help carry out His plan That view may separate me from some who call themselves Christians, but I don't think it separates me from Jesus Christ.

Long before the time of Jesus *my God* revealed Himself to all who would listen to Him. He continues to do so to this day. Many have accepted and shared the message they understood to come from God and acted in accordance with it. The Old Testament records many occasions during the eighteen hundred years of Jewish history leading to the birth of Jesus when God communicated with those important to Him and predicted the coming of a Messiah, the one "anointed" to save the Jews from their trials and tribulations.

If you know the spiritual qualities and teachings of Jesus Christ,

I believe you also know *my God*. Jesus was the very first human who not only listened and acted on *my God's* word, but by John's baptism also welcomed *my God* to do His will through him. God accepted that invitation and became one with Jesus to accomplish His will in our world. Jesus Christ set a new example for a relationship with God. Like all humans endowed with free will, Jesus could have ignored His will even after *my God* became one with him.

What distinguishes Jesus Christ from those who came after him, and makes him worthy of my worship, is that without question he never failed to accept God's will made known to him, even until his death. That was extraordinary at the very least and some would even consider it miraculous in a world of imperfect humans. Humanity may long remember his words and deeds, but I think his greatest legacy was the example he set by inviting *my God* to work through him and submitting totally to *my God's* will.

Christians often hear it said that "Christ died for our sins," but that is not fundamental to my acceptance of Jesus Christ. It carries a clear implication that physical death is bad even though everything that has ever lived has experienced it. It also infers that only through acceptance of Jesus Christ can one achieve oneness with God and an eternal life accompanying it. At the very least I question what that implies for those preceding Jesus who were totally faithful to *my God*.

The concept of Jesus as a Savior is not fundamental to my faith even though I believe God was revealed through Jesus Christ. I know the Jews of the Old Testament were hoping for a Messiah to "save" them from oppression, but Christians are asked to believe they have been "saved" from past sins of others as well as their own.

Bishop Spong writes "One cannot fall into sin from a perfection that one never possessed. One cannot be rescued from a fall that never happened. One cannot be restored to a status that one has never possessed, so the way we talk about salvation has become irrelevant"

I struggle with the concept of Jesus born from a virgin as the "Son of God," but I can well understand that because his ministry on earth took place two thousand years ago, Jesus had to speak the language of his time and place in order to convey God's Word. *My God* can make Himself understood to all of humanity, but Jesus was speaking to impressionable and largely illiterate human beings who were accustomed to hearing explanations containing figures of speech. They did not understand how invisible air was vital to their very being, and the concept of an invisible spiritual reality equally vital to life was surely beyond comprehension. They could, however, understand God as a father image to all who accepted Him.

Religions who welcome other sinners may well deny me welcome for such admissions but none of these doubts keep me from accepting Jesus Christ as the incarnation of *my God*. I simply do not think it is necessary to believe all that established Christian dogma requires me to believe in order to accept this. That said, I take no issue with established dogma if others find it helpful to believe it and *my God's* will is thereby accomplished.

Jesus said "Follow me," and it is important to me that, like Christ, I cooperate with *my God* by inviting Him to inhabit me and do His will through me. There have no doubt been many persons who made a greater contribution than I to achieve His will, and I have surely demonstrated plenty of imperfection, but I am counting on His forgiveness if I could have done more and did not.

Forgiveness is emphasized more in the New Testament than the Old, and I believe one of Jesus' greatest legacies is to help us understand that *my God* is a constant God. Forgiveness of those who repent for past offenses against Him and forgiveness of those who try to serve Him and fail has been fundamental to His nature for time eternal, long before the ministry of Jesus Christ. I think He wants us to emulate His forgiveness by learning to forgive others and ourselves as well.

Jesus was criticized during his ministry for presuming to forgive sins on behalf of God. He was in my view simply proclaiming God's nature to forgive all sins and thereby make them part of the past. *My God's* focus is always on achieving His ultimate intention. He knows better than we the importance of putting the past behind us so we can help accomplish His plan for the future.

According to scripture Jesus told his disciples that he was preparing a special place for them in his Father's house (clearly a figure of speech) for persons who please God. He also told them that only those who do the will of God shall enter Heaven. If *my God* decided to accomplish His will with the help of uniquely imperfect humans who ask His guidance, I do not understand why He would deprive us of Heaven simply because of our imperfection.

As I believe *my God* exists I believe Heaven also exists and I have no doubt that Heaven and God are inseparable. As with *my God* I think of Heaven as a spiritual reality rather than a physical place. Whether we go to Heaven or Heaven comes to us is an open question for me, as is whether we have to wait until we die to find Heaven. Many in life have already discovered *my God's* infinite love and the inner peace that comes from a relationship with Him.

Chapter Seven

Cooperating With My God

There are surely many ways to cooperate with my God's *plan.*

Adherents of Islam, Judaism and Christianity believe in God, trace their faith back to Abraham and claim their faith is based upon revelations from God, but there are distinct inconsistencies between them that cannot possibly be explained by any intention on my God's part to provide ambiguous guidance to different people. Surely the inconsistencies result either from imperfect understanding of His revelations, imperfect communication of them by those who profess to be His messengers, or loss of message clarity between the time the revelations were communicated by Him and the time they were documented for contemporary society.

It should come as no surprise that some who profess to be His messengers knowingly use His name to validate actions *my God* does not condone. This violates His commandment revealed to Moses that He will not hold guiltless those who take His name in vain.

I believe if you are looking for God a good place to find Him is in the Holy Bible. Muslims obviously believe He can be found in the Qur'an, and I have insufficient knowledge to quarrel with that.

I do quarrel with those who believe God can be found *only* in the Bible or Qur'an, and I do not accept the inerrancy of either book. The authors may have had the best of intentions, but they were no doubt just as imperfect as the rest of us, and I consider it unlikely that *my God* would have communicated with greater clarity to them than to others who came after them. They surely would have benefited from much that is known today that was unknown when the Bible and Qur'an were written and the languages used in the original books are all but obsolete in today's world. Much has, no doubt, been lost in translation into today's modern languages.

It is difficult to achieve near-octogenarian status and not notice along the way that certain practitioners of all faiths are inclined to use their own particular version of the written word of God to achieve ends useful to them. They may have perfectly rational reasons, such as simply wanting to stay employed, or choosing to believe what they have been taught to believe. Others may have reasons that are more sinister. When that happens, *my God's* eternal plan can suffer negative consequences, at least for a while.

My God was in Jesus Christ and the words and deeds of Jesus during his ministry reflected His wishes. If the four Gospels Matthew, Mark, Luke, and John, written starting forty years after the death of Jesus, were intended to convey those words and deeds, some message clarity appears to have been lost and no one is more persuasive in pointing out the contradictions than Bishop Spong. Even in our modern enlightened society it is very challenging for imperfect humans to accurately communicate an intended message to a diverse and equally imperfect audience and, except possibly for John, the Gospel writers were not even first-hand witnesses.

The writings of Paul between 51 and 64 CE do not support the idea of a physical resurrection. Mark, chronologically the first Gospel written in the early eighth decade by a scribe to Peter with access to Peter's personal recollection of actual events, tells the Easter story without ever once recording a narrative of the risen Christ appearing to anyone. Matthew, written some twelve years later and clearly expanding on the writings of Mark, describes the virgin birth and the physical appearances of Jesus Christ after the resurrection.

Bishop Spong appears to view Mark as more literal than Matthew, which he considers an *interpretive portrait* of the birth, death and resurrection of Jesus Christ. It is axiomatic that in order to inform and persuade, writers need to identify the nature of their potential readership and approach them in a manner that will encourage them to actually read and consider what has been written. Thanks to Bishop Spong's clarification, I find nothing to criticize in the discrepancies between Matthew and Mark but I wonder why, when the New Testament was assembled, an interpretative version would have been placed ahead of an earlier and more literal version.

Bishop Spong believes the Gospel writers, who were all Jews versed in the traditions of the Old Testament, told their version of the story in the ways they felt would best persuade Jews that Jesus Christ was anointed by God to be their Messiah. He points out that words attributed to Jesus during his time of passion mimic almost verbatim words contained in the Old Testament, particularly the 22nd Psalm and II Isaiah, and the Jews of the first century would have been comfortable with that because they knew the books of the Old Testament often were not meant to be taken literally. That understanding was lost starting late in the second century when Gentiles who knew less about the Old Testament became the primary interpreters of Gospel material. I think many more in today's informed and questioning world could be drawn to Jesus Christ if they were not expected to believe the literal truth of all that is contained in the New Testament.

Because He is without physicality and possesses perfect humility, *my God* can best accomplish His will through individuals who turn to Him, but as I discuss later in this work, He appears also to be influenced by prayer on behalf of others. It would appear obvious that *my God* cannot respond to anyone who denies His existence and refuses to turn to Him.

There is a vital role that spiritual leaders play in bringing humanity to a personal relationship with their God, but I question the sufficiency of communicating with God only through spiritual leaders. He is no doubt pleased when spiritual leaders acquire superior knowledge of His nature and written Word. I think spiritual leaders who possess that knowledge are best qualified to explain God to those who wish to know Him better and assist humanity to better understand Him, communicate with Him through prayer, and act in accordance with His response. They are not as well qualified as the individuals themselves to communicate individual needs to *my God*, but He surely listens and acts when they ask Him to be with those in need. He is no doubt displeased when persons who purport to be spiritual leaders knowingly elaborate upon or misinterpret His written word for personal temporal benefit.

Reason would indicate that *my God* communicates best with those who reach out to Him first, because in those circumstances there is both readiness and willingness to listen for a response. Those who do reach out to Him should respect that He responds on a schedule and in a manner that will most effectively further His plan for the world. Those who have placed their faith in Jesus Christ are able to discern *my God's* response when it occurs because it will conform to the spiritual qualities revealed in Jesus.

They are also able to accept that His response is in furtherance of His plan and not necessarily what they in their imperfect judgment were expecting.

Chapter Eight

Believers and Non-Believers

Implementation of my God's plan may suffer occasional setbacks and require reaction by Him to events outside His control, including physical events resulting from the Big Bang and free-willed activity of a diverse humanity.

Over my lifetime I have witnessed diminished reliance upon established Judeo-Christian religions in Europe and North America and increased priority placed on expediency and relative truth. *My God's* existence does not depend on whether or not people deny Him or, for that matter, upon His popularity at any point in time and in any particular place. Those who welcome Him into their lives will find Him and those who refuse will not.

The population of those faithful to *my God* in other parts of the world is, by all accounts, growing in number, and when they seek His guidance I believe it will be provided to them. Africa and South America will no doubt be increasingly important in carrying out His plan. I don't expect *my God* to ever stop His efforts to enlist humanity in carrying out His plan.

The churches and cathedrals in Europe are quite empty of worshipers, but I think *my God's* plan relies upon humanity carrying out His will in our physical world and not on temporary structures, as magnificent as they may be. They functioned efficiently since the Middle Ages as places to learn about and worship God and remain the best means of communicating His existence to people who gather together in order to better know Him and work together in carrying out His will.

The general population is far better educated today and other methods of communication not involving gathering in physical structures can communicate His existence very effectively. Houses of worship will never cease to be places to find *my God*, and to treat them as other than sacred would appear to deny Him, but His spirit pervades His entire domain and those looking for Him will always find Him no matter where they happen to be.

It is arguably true that some Western atheists and agnostics are no longer content to simply disbelieve but additionally try to create roadblocks for those who wish to practice faith. Some say that atheists demand a higher standard of proof for belief than for disbelief, and I agree.

This may be a reaction to past and present damage done in the name of God, and they may wonder why, if God exists, He would allow His followers to do such things. It might help for those disbelievers to consider that many who profess to act in the name of *my God* are knowingly doing so to achieve personal benefit, do not understand His nature, and have little interest in serving Him. It may also help to consider the possibility of a God who intervenes only by influencing those who would carry out his ultimate intention and who began only four thousand years ago to communicate His evolving requirements to humanity.

Many who act in the name of God have not personally invited Him into their lives and are under the influence of others who may claim to speak for God but do not. Agnostics and atheists may deny *my God* for themselves, but there is nothing they can do to change the reality of His existence.

Anyone who has faith in *my God* and opens the door to Him when He knocks will have His guidance in carrying out His will. All He asks is for them to act in accordance with that guidance as they truly perceive it and He will forgive them if they fall short. Achieving His will may take time and require patience and perseverance. Often significant sacrifice will be needed and progress will be difficult to discern. Often progress can be reversed when actions contrary to His will are performed by persons possessing free will but not His guidance. *My God's* plan for Creation is an eternal one and does not depend upon progress being made on any particular schedule. I think He can tolerate setbacks and move on.

Some atheists concede that religion can bring about good things, including art, music, charities, good works, wisdom, scripture, human fellowship, and togetherness, but these concessions are more than offset by atheist belief that religion gets people to live their lives based on something untrue, stops them from thinking rationally, prevents them from being self-reliant, imposes irrational rules of behavior, divides people and causes conflict and war.

Such accusations may indeed contain elements of truth with regard to many religions and individuals who practice them, but they do not reflect on His very existence. Nor do they justify begrudging less than perfect demonstrations of faith by those faithful to Him, or explain why atheists who deny God for themselves should presume to deny Him for others.

G. K. Chesterton said of people who don't believe in God that rather than believing in nothing, they believe in anything. A particularly harsh comment by Chesterton, but perhaps he was concerned that, without God, there is no common standard for good and bad.

Chapter Nine

The Taking of Life

Achievement of my God's plan for our world is inextricably linked to the availability of humanity to carry it out for Him.

Even among those who claim to be faithful to God, there continues to be wide acceptance for killing those with whom one disagrees, those who stand in the way of one's objectives, and even those whose very entry into life might inconvenience someone who has helped create it.

All of human life has the potential to further *my God's* plan for creation and is precious to Him for that reason, even life that has not yet acknowledged and reached out to Him. It is never too late in life to take the opportunity to serve *my God* and His plan benefits whenever someone does. The taking of any human life that could serve Him deprives *my God* of a potential servant. The taking of new life that hasn't yet been offered the choice of serving or denying Him God is arguably an even worse violation against Him.

Those who profess to take human life in *my God's* name are violators, not implementers, of His will. Anyone who supports such violations through encouragement, coercion or persuasion is equally responsible. Such people are, in effect, declaring themselves as gods. I believe *my God*, and not just man, will judge them. There is nothing humankind can do to change that reality, including the implementation of earthly laws intended to permit taking of human life, even under narrowly proscribed circumstances.

Leaders of today's so-called radical Islamic movement advocate the taking of life in God's name, but *my God* couldn't possibly countenance the deliberate taking of human life with ability to serve Him. The ancient Arabic written language contained in the Qur'an is understood today by only a few scholars and some of them have knowingly misinterpreted it to achieve and remain in power. They do great harm to His continuing creation and they have no place in eternity with *my God*.

If, as I believe, God communicates to and through all who reach out to Him, he surely communicated His will to Muhammad when he reached out to Him. I refuse to believe a God who relies upon humanity would countenance murder. If the Qur'an can be interpreted to permit murder I believe God's message became distorted either when Muhammad, who was reportedly illiterate, dictated God's message to his scribes or during subsequent translation of ancient Arabic into the modern.

Humanity is *my God's* only means for achieving His will in our physical world. He has uniquely chosen us not only because we are the most advanced species, but also because we alone have the ability to build upon the accomplishments of our predecessors. Individual human life is temporary, but humanity will exist for as long as *my God* judges it necessary for carrying out His will.

Spiritual life is eternal and physical life is finite, so lifespan is not as important to *my God* as accomplishment of His will. What is extremely important to Him is that a human life unnecessarily cut short deprives Him of the opportunity to use it to serve His purposes. For that reason human life should be defended vigorously from its very beginning until the time it can no longer serve *my God* in any way. The taking of one human life to protect another may be defensible, but preemptive taking of any human life is surely contrary to His will. There is no place in eternity for anyone who deliberately ignores *my God's* will made known to them and pre-emptively takes human life or coerces others to do so.

Three billion years ago life was created in our world, and since that time it has been extraordinary for individual life of any kind to survive one hundred years. Simple math tells us that more than one hundred million generations of life have existed since the creation of life itself. All of that life needed to die in order to provide organic matter vital to the survival and advancement of today's humanity.

I think the entirety of life as it has evolved, recreated itself and adapted to its environment over three billion years is what is vitally important to *my God*. This includes not only human life as the instrument of His will but other life that has in the past or will in the future have either a direct or indirect purpose in support of humanity. All life has enjoyed a unique and generous existence, even the life that served only as part of the food chain. As *my God* cares for and makes use of human lives who would serve His intention, I believe He expects humanity to do the same with all life over which it holds dominion.

I view longevity with the perspective of the many millions of generations preceding us, a world population of seven billion, and what God could accomplish with each life. Jesus never reached his thirty-third birthday, and his ministry only lasted three years, but He accomplished great things during his life.

Death is not something *my God* imposes on a case-by-case basis as individual punishment, nor can it be the end for those who are inhabited with His eternal spirit. In my view, those who have faith in *my God* and serve Him in physical life, should view as a loving gift the physical life they have been privileged to enjoy.

Chapter Ten

Miracles

Absence of belief in any God seems to correlate with disbelief in miracles, particularly those that relate to Judeo-Christian history. As a person of science I have difficulty believing in miracles but very much believe in my God.

Any incomprehensible and seemingly miraculous event that falls outside the accumulated knowledge and understanding of physical science is often dismissed for that reason alone. Even though science appears to have definitive knowledge of less than five per cent of our Universe and has to extrapolate from that knowledge to explain the remaining ninety-six.

There are no spiritual limits to what *my God* could accomplish, but having no physicality He would seem incapable of performing any physical acts, miraculous or not. I struggled much of my life to reconcile this physical limitation with what I had been taught to believe.

It is fundamental to my faith that my eternal and omniscient God existed at the time of the Big Bang and has absolute knowledge of the laws governing our physical universe and all that it will be at any point in time. It is not fundamental to my faith that He created the Big Bang by thinking it into existence, and if science one day should prove otherwise, my faith would not be shaken.

Even without physicality *my God* could use physical events for His own good purposes by inhabiting and influencing humanity as His physical presence. Seemingly miraculous things have no doubt been accomplished when His foreknowledge of extraordinary physical events was shared with persons faithful to Him. The rescue of the children of Israel from Pharaoh is surely a classic example of such an event. I find it instructive regarding how *my God* works that Moses was prepared over a lifetime for such a singular magnificent accomplishment.

The parting and closing of the Red Sea, or "Sea of Reeds" as some would believe, were timed propitiously to escape Pharaoh's army. Yet many today believe it was a predictable event recognizable to persons living locally. Moses had lived in the nearby wilderness in his early years. By observing where caravans crossed at low tide, he could well have known the ancient methods of predicting tides based on wind conditions and on the moon's phase and position in the sky. He also could have planned the Israelites' escape knowing when extreme low tide would occur, how long the sea bottom would remain dry and when the waters would rush back in.

When *my God* needed someone to lead the people of Israel He would no doubt have chosen someone with the life experience, accumulated knowledge, and ability of Moses. It was a "Moses moment in time" when he chose to reach out to and listen to *my God,* and was one of many for him. I suspect since that time many, who like Moses, choose to follow His guidance, experience their own "Moses moments in time."

Simply because something is scientifically inexplicable at any given point in time doesn't foreclose the possibility that it will be perfectly understood at a time in the future. There is much to be discovered in our Universe. New discoveries are occurring every day, and science continues to unravel the mysteries of the Universe.

The four Gospels record many seemingly miraculous acts Jesus performed, none of which the Gospel writers appear to have witnessed and many of which are simply repeated from Gospel to Gospel. I do not need to believe Jesus performed miracles in order to believe he was fully inhabited by God. The Gospel writers may well have believed as I do, but they had undertaken the enormous challenge of persuading people under very different circumstances than exist today that the true God was revealed in Jesus.

They surely needed a dramatic story to attract the attention of their target audience, namely Jews. The story may well have been exaggerated by the Apostles or by others retelling the "good news" during the forty years leading up to writing the first Gospel. Judging by the inconsistencies between them, it might even have been exaggerated by the Gospel writers themselves.

The Gospels are replete with stories of Jesus' amazing healing powers, and one does not need to believe in miracles to accept that many such events actually happened. Countless inexplicable medical "miracles" have occurred over history and I believe there are no limits to what can be accomplished by my infinite God working through those He inhabits. Healing in its broadest sense is surely the greatest expression of *my God's* compassion for humankind, and even for those who have not yet placed faith in Him. All who are so healed, might well consider it as an opportunity to serve Him in the remaining days they have been given.

If miracles are defined as events that are now and may forever remain incomprehensible to humankind, four such "miracles" come to mind. All are, at the very least, remarkable, but none is fundamental to my belief in *my God*.

First, the prelude and creation of the Big Bang. Science is

increasing its understanding of the aftermath of the Big Bang, but it may never have the capacity to comprehend how a Universe more than 26 billion light-years across, containing more than one hundred billion galaxies, started before the existence of time itself as virtually nothing. A Universe that could not have sustained itself if it had chosen to expand at a rate one millionth less or one millionth more than the rate it is expanding. A Universe that makes more and more sense with every new discovery by the most brilliant scientists our planet has produced.

Second, the origin of life. Scientists have determined that the formation of our solar system and planet date back some 4.4 billion years. Life in its simplest form coming some 1 billion years later, and has further determined that fundamental *organic* life capable of replicating itself arose from *inorganic* physical matter via natural chemical reaction. To my knowledge, the chemical process that caused this is not understood by science and may well never be.

Third, the evolution of life. Emerging from its fundamental origin into an incredibly diverse community of life forms, all needed to achieve *my God's* plan for our world and even beyond. This ongoing process involves an incomprehensible number of life forms coming into and going out of existence, reproducing, living, dying and adapting over time to specific and varying environments. A survival instinct fundamental to life since its origin no doubt contributed to this evolution, but humankind may never fully comprehend its complexities.

Finally, the emergence of a human species. Comprised of self-determined life forms possessing unique and diverse life experience and unique levels of physical ability, intelligence, creativity, industriousness and reasoning. Endowed with varying degrees of wisdom, compassion, humility, justice, mercy, forgiveness and understanding, the human species has worked individually and collectively to create enormous common good. Evolution of the human life form is not diminished by those who use their gifts in selfish and destructive ways. They, like all of us, eventually pass from the scene and *my God's* work can recommence without them.

The resurrection of Jesus Christ from his brutal death was not the only such return from death reported in the Bible, and it is certainly curious that the Gospels report various occasions when Jesus was not physically recognizable until he spoke. I understand many theologians today privately question the reality of this important cornerstone of the Christian faith.

In the April 23, 2015 post on his weekly blog *A New Christianity for a New World*, Bishop Spong asks:

"If the resurrection is to be regarded by 21st century believers as a literal event that actually happened in time, in space and in history, why are the details surrounding the description of that event in the Bible so filled with contradictions? Are we sufficiently aware of the biblical stories of the resurrection to know that they disagree on such basic questions as who went to the tomb, what did they see, who was the first to discern Jesus as raised from the dead, and where were the disciples when Easter dawned on their consciousness? Do we realize that even that location is disputed in the gospels? How could the same resurrected body that walked through locked doors in one gospel also in that same gospel be probed physically by the hands of Thomas? Can a body capable of appearing and disappearing also do such physical things as eating, drinking, talking, walking and interpreting scripture? Are we aware that no one saw the risen Jesus in Mark's gospel; they only got a promise that they would see him in Galilee? Are we aware that Galilee was a seven to ten day journey from Jerusalem?"

Bishop Spong further writes in his blog post of May 14, 2015: "What did the Christian movement know about the resurrection of Jesus before the first gospel was written in the eighth decade of the Christian era? The answer to that question is 'not very much.' The only records between 30 CE, the date of the crucifixion, and 72 CE, the date of the writing of the first gospel, are found in the writings of Paul between 51 and 64 CE. From Paul we learned first that the resurrection of Jesus was always spoken of in the passive tense [indicating] that originally resurrection was thought of as an act of God being applied to Jesus, not an act of Jesus in charge of his own destiny. Paul believed that the raised Jesus had 'appeared' to certain chosen witnesses [and] the Greek word that has been translated does not necessarily refer [to] the seeing of an objective reality. It is a word that could also be translated 'was revealed to' or 'was made manifest to.' Since Paul's conversion is today believed to have happened anywhere from one to six years after the crucifixion we must conclude that what Paul saw was not a physical body.

'The first thing that one notices about Mark is that this original gospel's story of Easter is incredibly brief, even stark. It is only eight verses long. Many early Christians found it so lacking in details that more than one wrote a new ending for this gospel. Two of those 'new' endings were later incorporated into the text of Mark itself and they even appeared as part of Mark's gospel in the King James Version of the Bible. Most modern translations of Mark's gospel have dropped everything after Mark 16:8 into a footnote or they have separated 16:9-20 from 16:1-8 by a space and say in the footnotes that these verses 'cannot have been part of the original text of Mark.' A cursory reading of these verses reveals that they were an attempt to harmonize Mark's gospel with the texts of the later gospels. So, if we are going to be faithful to our stated task of examining what the New Testament literally says about the resurrection of Jesus, we must go next to only Mark 16:1-8, the second witness to the resurrection, in the New Testament."

Even though it appears second in the New Testament, the Gospel of Mark was the first to be written, and its author is generally acknowledged not only as a student of the Apostle Peter, but also his scribe. Those facts provide me greater comfort in his Gospel compared to other three, but I think Bishop Spong has the last word on the resurrection in his blog of June 11, 2015.

> "For Matthew God is not a noun that we must define. God is a verb that must be lived. This was Matthew's truth, inside which he wrapped his Gospel. Jesus was the symbol of the God who is with us, the God who is Emmanuel. The angel said to Joseph in a dream that Emmanuel means God with us. The final word of Matthew's Christ to Matthew's readers is, 'Lo, I am with you always. I am the ultimate promise of God. You live in me; I live in you.' That is what resurrection ultimately means."

Chapter Eleven

Science and My God

Many people of science consider themselves inventive persons capable of original scientific accomplishment.

I now realize that, rather than being inventive, I have been a discoverer of things that already existed. My only accomplishments have been to make such things known and produce some benefit from what I discovered.

What I and others have accomplished may have at times taken unique intelligence, knowledge and talent at the right time and place to further *my God's* plan, but it should be self-evident that no person can claim to have invented something from absolutely nothing. We made use of our unique capabilities to discover things previously unknown. Things that may have greatly advanced our civilization, but without question whatever we discovered was a product of the Big Bang and was already present and waiting to be discovered.

Any person of science needs to face the reality that, at best, his or her knowledge of the Big Bang is limited to the small part of its aftermath already discovered and he or she has no idea whatsoever of what remains to be discovered in our Universe. Scientists have arguably discovered only a minute percentage of what remains to be discovered, and much of what science already thinks it knows, is, in any event, based on consensus and not universally accepted truth.

It is troubling that the work of many persons of science causes them to move away from belief in *my God's* existence. Many atheists base their own disbelief on these convictions, but a scientist's knowledge is limited to what has either been taught or observed of the physical universe, so a scientist is no more qualified than anyone else to comment on *my God's spiritual* existence.

Knowledge that has not yet been revealed to science but someday will be, is obviously outside a scientist's expertise and new scientific discoveries are happening every day. Scientists always ought to qualify their opinions on religious matters by prefacing them with "based upon what is currently known to be scientific fact," and their opinions are, in any event, just that. An individual scientist's opinion is based on what is known to him or her of the physical universe, but much more is known only to others, much more will be made known in the future, and much that is incomprehensible today may or may not remain so forever.

My God is unseen, infinite and eternal and no scientist worthy of that name can claim that all of existence is visible, finite and temporal. Those scientists who deny His existence and the atheists who rely on them need to recognize the shaky ground on which they are standing.

In his book *The Grand Design,* Stephen Hawking question's God's role as Creator of our Universe and further opines that our Universe seems to be one of many, each with different laws. I've read some of his work and can't pretend to understand all that he and other astrophysicists have to say. Hawking is no doubt the preeminent astrophysicist of our time and perhaps he is moving away from belief in a higher existence because he thinks God's enormity could not possibly encompass an infinite number of universes. Stephen Hawking may well be the most intelligent person our planet has produced, but the extent of *my God's* infinite and eternal spiritual reality is arguably incomprehensible to him also. Is it possible that even Stephen Hawking isn't thinking *big* enough?

Infinity, by definition, has no limits, so why should anyone think only in terms of a visible Universe that is a *mere* 26 billion light years in diameter when that is in itself a limit? Indeed, why would anyone rule out the possibility of an infinite number of big bangs and an infinite number of resulting universes, each with different laws?

Our world is special to *my God,* but His domain is infinite and there is no reason to believe it is limited to our universe, much less our galaxy or world.

Science to date appears to have definitive proof only of the ordinary matter and energy contained in our Universe, and that is less than 5% of what they know is needed in order for the Universe to make scientific sense. While progress is being made, so-called dark matter, said to comprise 23% of the Universe, and dark energy, said to comprise 73%, have not yet been isolated and are not yet well understood.

The Universe has been expanding away from the Big Bang for 14 billion years and the region of the Universe visible from earth is reported by science as containing more than 100 billion galaxies and 3 sextillion (3 with 21 zeros after it) stars. Even without adding the planets, etc. captured by each star's gravitational system, as well as satellites encircling the planets, these numbers are clearly incomprehensible to humanity. That is only the visible part of our Universe. A significant part of the Universe moving away from us at the speed of light may well not be discernible from earth and may never be in the future. If so, science has no choice but to expect that part of our Universe to behave in a similar manner to the visible, but as with dark energy and dark matter, there is no scientific proof now nor probably ever.

The physical world where Hawking and the scientific community dwell demands physical scientific evidence supporting *my God's* existence. However, the entirety of human accomplishment provides compelling physical evidence, and the artificiality of the "rules of evidence" established by science stand in the way of recognizing it. *My God* has no physicality and insistence on physical evidence ignores any possibility of a spiritual world coexistent with the physical.

Many thoughtful, intelligent people are no less qualified than Hawking and other persons of science to comprehend the incomprehensible, including dark matter, dark energy, the invisible side of our own universe and the enormity of a spiritual and eternal being existent throughout our own universe and others as well.

As brilliant as he may be, even Stephen Hawking is infinitely distant from any ability to disprove *my God's* existence. In *The Grand Design,* Hawking refutes the traditional Christian belief regarding existence of "an intelligent natural world that functions according to some deliberate design." His follow-up conclusion is that the absence of a Grand Design eliminates any need for a *benevolent creator.* I think Hawking fails to recognize that His creation may well have started with the Big Bang and, rather than our needing Him to serve us, *my God* needs humanity to serve Him and carry out His will. Even Stephen Hawking cannot comprehend *my God's* infinite, eternal and pervasive reality. Since *my God* has no physicality, Stephen Hawking will never find Him if he looks only at the physical universe. As with all of humanity, if he seeks *my God* spiritually, he will find Him. He may have to set aside his some of his great analytical skills to do that.

While science knows a great deal about the aftermath of the Big Bang, to my knowledge no one, including Hawking, knows anything about how the Big Bang was made to happen. My faith does not require me to believe *my God* created the Big Bang, and if some day science has another explanation for its origin, my faith in Him will not suffer. The bedrock of my belief is that *my God* knows all there is to know about the natural course of the Big Bang and has a wish to influence its outcome that humanity, with His help, can accomplish. Some might call that a Grand Design.

My God has no physical ability to micromanage events or outcome and instead all of humanity is endowed with free will and creative ability so we can do it for Him. Rather than waving a wand to make it happen it is *my God's* wish that the end result of the Big Bang will be influenced by humanity who look to Him for spiritual guidance. Those who choose not to look to Him may influence the process but not the final outcome. Time is on His side.

My omniscient God knew in advance that there would someday exist a place in the Universe hospitable to life, that basic life would be created where none existed, and that humankind would emerge as an intelligent life form ready for Him to reveal Himself. He decided long ago to involve humankind as His principal resource in carrying out His Grand Design, and that is part of what makes us so special.

Researchers studying subatomic particles with the help of the CERN particle physics laboratory in Europe appear to have isolated the Higgs boson, the missing piece that completes the so-called Standard Model, claimed to be the smallest and most fundamental component in everything contained in our Universe. They apparently believe this Standard Model is the basic building block in the atomic structure of all identified elements known to possibly exist in our Universe and the most convincing explanation available for the way the Universe works in all of its aspects except gravity.

Judging by its nickname, the "God particle," it seems that some believe His very essence can be found in the Higgs boson. *My God's* spirit pervades all of the Universe, including each and every Higgs boson.

Chapter Twelve

The Imperfection of Humankind

Even Jesus acknowledged pervasive imperfection in our world and it is certainly reasonable to ask why any God would chose a humankind that is individually and collectively imperfect to carry out His Grand Design.

Aside from the obvious answer that we may be all He has to work with, we could not possibly be perfect unless we were all identical, making things pretty boring for us and for Him. Not to mention that if humankind were perfect we would be His equal and not His servant, bringing into question our purpose in my God's world. All of life, particularly humankind, is still evolving and cannot possibly be perfect for that reason alone, and I think the explanation is more fundamental.

Starting fourteen million years ago, the Big Bang created something from absolutely nothing, a process that continues to this day. Life in our world began its own evolutionary process three billion years ago, and that process is, by its very nature, a completion of something that started out as incomplete; in other words, a perfecting process. It has taken place on an individual basis by members of humanity who are still evolving, and it should be no surprise that each of us is uniquely imperfect at every point in time. We are definitely not there yet, and *my God's* plan is arguably best accomplished by a near infinite variety of intellectual, creative, and physical abilities.

I am intrigued not only by the possibility that my purely spiritual God chose to inhabit humanity to carry on Creation, but also by the reality that His chosen are each uniquely imperfect. Some of the "imperfect" explanations that have occurred to me include:

- Perhaps *my God* is creating over time a physical world that mirrors the perfection of His spiritual world and this involves a perfecting process because it started from absolutely nothing. The evolutionary process for each member of humankind has been, by its very nature, unique, but in the world He wishes to perfect, humankind may well become collectively perfect. Humans with a variety of physical, creative, and intellectual capabilities, all having their own life experiences, may be the best way to achieve *my God's* Creation. It would be more interesting for Him and also for humanity. Some great thinkers characterize the use of uniquely imperfect persons to carry out His will as "God's Play."

- Perhaps, without ever having seen or experienced perfection, it is impossible for humankind to contemplate or define it. But in the context of imperfection, perfection can be thought of as an ideal ultimate objective of *my God's* will for His world. Similarly, His ongoing Creation is a process of perfecting something that started with the Big Bang and that over the eons will be made perfect with the help of humanity.

- The human life form has clearly evolved in a very positive way over the 3 billion years since the origin of life. Except for adapting to environmental changes, no other known life form has experienced comparable improvement in creativity, physical ability, and intellectual capability. Human evolution thus far has not been in the direction of individual perfection, or even collective perfection, and probably *my God* is content for humanity to carry out His will in our physical world in an imperfect manner. He would nonetheless like humankind to communicate with Him, do its imperfect best to understand and carry out what He communicates, recognize our own imperfection, and even take our imperfection into account in our actions.

I have heard many explanations for the doctrine of "original sin," including the opinion of many Christian leaders that it is something that existed before we were born and that we need to atone for, including the purely symbolic sin of Adam and Eve. Bishop Spong would appear to deny original sin in its entirety. Maurice Boyd was fond of saying that evil is universal, pervasive and intractable and that the doctrine of original sin comes down to "Nothing is as it should be." He usually followed that up with "Nothing need stay the way it is." He often referred to original sin as a "cheerful doctrine," perhaps thinking we have no way to go but up.

I find comfort in Maurice Boyd's point of view and much prefer to spend my limited days cooperating with *my God* to achieve good out of bad than to spend them apologizing for an imperfect world that existed long before I came into it. *My God* prefers to look forward rather than back, and those who accept Him might think of His plan for our world as perfecting the aftermath of the Big Bang through the use of humanity that seeks His guidance.

In my view, the tragic natural physical events that from time to time create challenges for humankind are associated only with the natural physical evolution of the Big Bang. They were predestined long before life existed and are not the result of any intention on *my God's* part to punish humanity for its imperfection.

Finally, individual free will and perfection are mutually exclusive. Individual free will has been needed in order to accomplish *my God's* plan, and the accompanying human imperfection, some of which is very damaging, has been a necessary part of the process. *My God* may try to minimize that damage by spiritual intervention, but individual free will sometimes shuts Him out. The Big Bang might have taken place fourteen billion years ago, but the human life form has been around for four million years and only acquired the ability to reason 200,000 years ago. My patient God has plenty of time.

Chapter Thirteen

Heaven

Many think of Heaven as a place we go to when we die, and of course many believe that no such place exists.

Maurice Boyd often spoke of Heaven as a place from which we come when we are born and to which we return when we die. The hard truth is that until we die, we will not know whether a heaven exists for us or indeed for anyone.

People who have experienced near-death describe a heaven they visited and then returned from as very beautiful and serene. None claim to have seen God but all seem ready to accept His existence.

Accepting *my God* as a spiritual, infinite and eternal reality coexisting with, encompassing, and permeating our physical Universe has led me to think of Heaven more as a concept rather than a place, and that gives me great comfort. If there is no physicality to Heaven there is no place to point to in order to locate it. That would be like trying to point your finger toward the ocean when you are immersed and surrounded by it as far as the eye can see. Looking up, down, left, right, front, back, and then inside ourselves might be a better way to think of it. Of course, we will still not see it but perhaps with His help we can start to believe it is there and prepare for it during life.

Perhaps *my God* and Heaven are one and the same: a pervasive spiritual reality where He exists that some may choose to take into themselves during life and some may not. Perhaps physical life gives us the opportunity to become one with *my God* and Heaven while we are alive, and that opportunity is lost to us when we die. Perhaps we *achieve* Heaven during life, and perhaps the Heaven we achieve varies with the degree to which we welcome Him into our lives. That would help explain why some might be denied Heaven. They and not *my God* were the deniers.

Perhaps Heaven comes to us when we invite *my God* into our very being. In my view, Heaven is not a place to "go to," or even a "place," because those words denote physicality. It is a purely spiritual reality where *my God's* presence can be found by those who seek Him; a reality to prepare for and even cherish during time on earth. Perhaps when He stands at the door and knocks and we choose to open the door we are inhabited by a spiritual part of Him that is as unique to each of us as our physical reality. Perhaps it is what has been called our eternal "soul." As Maurice Boyd used to say, you don't *have* a soul, you *are* a soul.

I question why those who have had every opportunity in life to seek *my God* and have nevertheless denied Him should expect to be part of His eternal reality. Perhaps anyone who invites my God into his or her life and repents for past actions continues to know Him after death even if they have not particularly pleased Him. They may displease Him, but He epitomizes forgiveness and they are inseparable from His compassionate love.

My God is incapable of imposing His own punishment on those who reach out to Him and nevertheless displease Him. There may indeed be punishment, but it will be self-imposed and commensurate with failure to please Him when we had the opportunity. Eternal knowledge that He exists, how much we fell short of what we might have accomplished during life, and the resulting consequences to His plan will in themselves be significant punishment when the time comes.

Notwithstanding His infinite love and forgiveness, there is a personal spiritual burden to be borne for failure to please Him. I believe that burden will be inescapable, self-imposed, commensurate and eternal. Christians are taught that the burden can be lessened by recognition and meaningful action taken in true repentance during our time on earth. After death it is too late, and those who deliberately deprive others of life as their last living act or coerce others to do so should have no eternal expectations with *my God*.

My God expects imperfection in those who have faith in Him. When they attempt to carry out His will made known to them, He is equally pleased whether they succeed or fail. That said, even those faithful to Him are capable of knowingly and deliberately violating His will, and for that they need to repent while there is time.

Chapter Fourteen

Prayer and *My God's* Humility

There are persons who spend every waking moment of their lives praying to God and trying to serve Him, and there is plenty of evidence that many other persons can go through life without ever involving God.

My life has fallen in the middle, and I suspect I have plenty of company. In my view I have led a unique life and possess a unique combination of creative, physical and intellectual capabilities. It has been my wish to use those capabilities to enjoy a secular life of my own choosing that includes accomplishing things I judge to be good. I mention elsewhere in this work that my standard for good and bad relates to *my God's* intention for our world.

I would like to think He is content for humans to utilize our unique gifts in pursuit of individual lives of our own choosing. I do not think He is content for us to interfere with others' enjoyment of lives they might use their own gifts to pursue, but He no doubt is pleased when we offer them assistance.

Nor do I think *my God* wishes to be either a micromanager or a spectator of life lived by a human species. There is surely an endless stream of unique situations where His will would benefit from unique combinations of life experience and physical, creative and intellectual qualities possessed by individuals committed to Him. He could perhaps choose to intervene with those individuals, but I believe that in His humility He prefers to accomplish His will through those who first welcome Him in.

All that is needed is for those endowed with free will to accept through faith that He has a plan that needs them, welcome Him into their lives, and offer Him their talents in pursuit of His wishes. *My God* has much to ask of those who turn to Him and He stands ready to communicate how each of us can play a part.

Prayer is not just for persons who have accepted Jesus Christ. *My God* will listen and respond to anyone who accepts the reality of His existence, communicates directly with Him through prayer, offers his or her unique talents to serve Him and endeavors to follow His guidance. Because Christians accept God's nature as it was revealed in Jesus, they may be more effective in communicating with God, but *my God* answers all prayers in His own way and on His own schedule.

My God does not personally perform anything in our physical world and instead provides guidance in carrying out His agenda as it exists at any point in time. That agenda is not a step-by-step process. He is constantly changing it in response to free-willed actions by both His faithful and those not faithful. He never loses sight, however, of His final intention for the world we inhabit.

His responses are often used productively to carry out His will, but it should be no surprise that they are often misunderstood and even ignored when understood. *My God's* limitless forgiveness goes hand in hand with His responses to those who come to Him in prayer.

Communal prayer serves an important role in bringing large elements of humanity closer to *my God*, but I think private communication with Him by prayer is the best way to show acceptance of His will for our world and understand how we might contribute our unique qualities in carrying it out. This is a major element of the Lord's Prayer taught by Jesus, which also adds a request for needed sustenance and forgiveness when we fall short. Private prayer provides something for Him to respond to on an individual basis and is crucial for carrying out His will in a manner He coordinates. Everyone can shoulder a level of responsibility in *my God's* world, and no responsibility is insignificant.

I view private prayer as the best way to determine what it is that He uniquely requires from us. I do not think He requires us to speak in order to be understood by Him and in my experience I have never heard a spoken word from Him. I have instead perceived thoughts coming into my mind after I have sought His guidance. I consider these responses originated in the mind of God, whether they come directly in the quiet of the night when my mind was open to them or indirectly by the spoken or written word of others. Responses that came indirectly were surely communicated with less precision because human imperfection intervened in the process.

I am quite sure when God communicated with humankind in the various recorded events of Judeo Christian and Muslim history he did so by communication through the mind and not the spoken word, and that His message was "perceived" and not heard. I am also quite sure that human imperfection has influenced what exists today as the written word of God but by reaching out to Him in private prayer humankind can discern His true intention.

He already knows better than us how we fit into His plan for our world and when He might require us. Beyond asking for His strength and wisdom, it would appear unproductive for humankind to determine the results it considers desirable and then ask

Him to provide them. This applies not only to the child who asks for a pony or a bicycle or to the athlete who prays to win a competitive event, but also to the person at life's end who asks for ten more years, weeks or even days. In my opinion, this also applies to the "peace in our time" that many people pray for, unless what is intended is the inner peace that comes from a relationship with Him. We are loved beyond comprehension, but *my God* is not our servant, and we are unaware of His intentions for our life and world.

This in no way rules out asking Him to provide wisdom and strength during times of need and adversity. He is always with us, but we need to ask in order for Him to respond and we need to accept that the outcome of our asking is in His hands.

My God provides guidance both to those who pray for themselves and those for whom prayers are offered. Asking Him to provide His guidance, wisdom and strength to others may well accomplish far more than prayer for oneself. It may also be very productive to ask Him through prayer to be with persons who are not our friend or even His friend. When problems seem beyond human solutions, He is the perfect choice to guide and assist those we love and those we find difficult to love.

Prayer to my humble God receives responses that epitomize compassion, wisdom, justice, mercy, forgiveness, understanding and patience. If those qualities are not in the discerned response, it is either not coming from Him or being distorted by our own prejudices or the influence of others.

He has two alternative means of intervening in our lives: communicating directly to us, or communicating with another who can in turn communicate His will to us or even take action on our behalf. I suspect most persons have no idea how frequently others pray for them or how much *my God* intervenes in their lives by influencing the actions of others.

We may well know our personal gifts and imperfections, but we do not know with certainty how or even whether they are useful to His will unless He communicates that to us. There may have been no instances of deep sonorous voices from the heavens for me, but there have been plenty of times when I sought His counsel in quiet privacy and discerned thoughts coming to mind either in the quiet of the night or through the lips of others who provided guidance. There have also been many actions by others, some barely known to me, that responded on a schedule not necessarily suiting my hope for prompt action but ultimately best suited to my needs and, I am sure, His needs.

It is pretty obvious not only that each of us is a unique combination of physical, intellectual and creative ability but that we also contribute uniquely every time we engage in life's activities. Free-willed activity of life not influenced by *my God,* often bad, is taking place constantly. He needs those who turn to Him to respond in a manner that serves His plan. He is far more qualified than we to determine when and how we can best do that. Free-willed activity of life not under *my God's* influence is a continuing thing, as is His need for us to reach out and respond to His guidance.

On the subject of deep sonorous voices from the heavens, the Old and New Testaments report occasions when God's word was heard, often by many. In Exodus God spoke to over two million people, and in the book of Acts one hundred persons communicated simultaneously to Him in their own tongue. Matthew tells how, following his death and resurrection, Jesus Christ spoke to the eleven at the Galilean mountaintop, a nine day journey from Jerusalem. His message, no doubt *my God's* message as well, was that all who are in the world are to know the love of God includes them also.

Surely any God with the ability to communicate simultaneously to such diverse groups also has the ability to communicate individually with anyone who reaches out to Him. My spiritual God is in constant communication with those faithful to Him in a clear manner that leaves no doubt it is coming from Him, and language is never a barrier. Billions of people speaking many languages are faithful to Him and in communication with Him. There are no limits on His ability to communicate with clarity on a great variety of subjects to a great variety of persons. Whether His sonorous voice is "perceived" in minds or "heard" through ears would appear irrelevant.

My God knows our needs better than we know them ourselves and epitomizes compassion, justice, mercy and forgiveness. Accepting that has helped me understand the Lord's Prayer taught by Jesus to his disciples, which, in my opinion, is too often recited with little thought or understanding by persons today.

For me the beginning of the prayer, "Our Father who art in Heaven, hallowed be Thy name," establishes and accepts the nature of the relationship as being a respectful one between man or woman and an unseen God. By saying "Thy kingdom come, Thy will be done on earth as it is in Heaven," we are stating our commitment to carry out His will for our world and to become more like Him. "Give us this day our daily bread" is a symbolic way to acknowledge that we are looking only to God for our spiritual needs, and "forgive us our debts as we forgive others" recognizes that forgiveness is our obligation and not just His gift. Finally, "lead us not into temptation but deliver us from evil" is our commitment that neither temptation nor evil will separate us from a relationship with Him.

We may not be petitioning anything specific by repeating the

Lord's Prayer, but we are preparing ourselves for a dialog with Him and inviting Him to join that dialog.

How we give voice to what we bring to *my God* in prayer is less important, because He knows all need and responds to need when invited even when we are unable to express it clearly. If we maintain a regular dialog with *my God* and conduct our lives in accordance with what we discern from that dialog, I believe we will serve Him well and He will be pleased.

Chapter Fifteen

Power in Service to *My God*

Maurice Boyd often asked "Where are you in your place of power?"

I think he saw in humanity a disposition to seek advantage by the pursuit and maintenance of power. In less polite terms, the powerful all too often feed upon the powerless.

Maurice considered power as the ability to achieve purpose. In my observation power is relative and important within and between various life forms and can be achieved through physical superiority, intellectual superiority, scientific superiority, economic superiority and/or superiority in numbers. Sadly, a level of ruthlessness helps as well. *My God* wants those who realize a place of power to use it to help achieve His ultimate intention.

Most of the world most of the time has lived under tyranny imposed by persons who ruthlessly achieved great power, gained enormous comfort and wealth on the backs of those they controlled and used that wealth to maintain control for a very long time. Throughout history tyranny has interfered with humanity's ability to serve God and is arguably evil for that reason alone. It functions most effectively when it is able to conjure up a bogus enemy and the current radical Islam is no exception.

Democracy in various forms evolved as an alternative to tyranny and America's founders chose a form of democracy that enabled those who wish to worship God to do so freely and individually. The ideal for all democratic forms of government is to convey power to those who would serve the public interest and replace those who fall short, but in our modern world even democracy is too often perverted by persons who instead abuse the trust placed in them to achieve personal enrichment. True public service, taking time out of life to contribute one's best abilities to advance the interests of those who trust one with power, was once routine in some democratic societies. It is exceptional today, and the democratic systems that have evolved make it difficult for those who try.

My God's will is well served by a power structure uniting the best capabilities of those who would serve him as leaders, followers, and those in between. It is not well served by those who realize a place of power to serve selfish needs contrary to His will. Financial systems important to the needs of a civilized society that could advance His ultimate intention are too often used only to enrich those with power to influence the system and its functioning. Those in trust routinely pursue financial advantage at the expense of the less enlightened, rather than serving them for mutual benefit, and the attitude appears to pervade the entire financial community. From my perspective capitalism could do a far better job in this regard.

A system of law and jurisprudence, created in the interest of ensuring justice and mercy fundamental to His nature, routinely pursues their avoidance or postponement to the benefit of participants knowledgeable of its intricacies. The system seems very much oriented toward ensuring reliance on an entrenched legal structure for life's activities and not enough about providing prompt and affordable justice for all who could benefit from it.

Western governments persist in imposing conflicted laws on top of one another, forsaking justice for power and making justice politicized, expensive, and virtually impossible to discern or achieve. Truth has become a relative question that is routinely compromised by those with ability to use the law to achieve personal ends. All too often the wealthy and powerful benefit to the detriment of those who have neither wealth nor power by delaying the process interminably when it suits them.

Our system of education is intended to prepare young people for the very greatest achievements their talents permit and enlightening all who thirst for knowledge, but it is too often used for achieving personal priorities of those in power and those with entrenched self-interest in the education process. Even healing of the sick, surely the noblest of professions, has arguably lost its way because of those who seek to achieve power or wealth by intervening in the process.

Over the ages religion has been a path to power for those who would pursue it, and Christianity is no exception. Persons of faith are particularly vulnerable to abuse of power by their leadership because trust is an important first element of faith. Great damage is done by Christian leaders who presume to know *my God's* will as only He knows it and then impose their personal will in His name or Jesus' to the detriment of many. It is equally true for those leaders of the Muslim community who, with the help of enormous oil wealth, choose to radicalize God's message to Muhammad, countenance evil in God's name and intimidate the impressionable and helpless into performing acts of unspeakable horror.

Bishop Spong writes that Christianity's call is never to collect power with which to rule the world, but rather to be a light in the world's darkness. *My God* wishes us to be His presence to all of life, not to rule it.

Chapter Sixteen

The Word of God

It is the custom in some churches I have attended for the congregation to recite "This is the Word of God" after the reading of a scriptural passage.

I understand those of the Jewish faith acknowledge the Torah as God's word and those of the Muslim faith similarly acknowledge God's presence after reciting the Qur'an. Reading from scripture usually sets the stage for a message of interpretation by a priest, minister, rabbi or imam and is a time-proven way for preachers to add relevance to their messages.

Over time, those who regularly attend worship also have the opportunity to understand more about the scriptures than they might otherwise absorb simply by reading them. For many, the "Word of God" best comes alive when it is explained by persons who can call on their superior knowledge of the full circumstances surrounding any particular scriptural event. There is no better reason to attend worship service than to listen to someone committed to delivering God's Word.

Bishop Spong points out that by reciting "This is the Word of God" we often do not notice, much less worry, about the contradictions, the variations, the additions and subtractions that are contained in scripture, and we also assume that the story was recorded in some pristine perfection. He writes, "If what has just been read is the word of God, we assume it must be accurate, perfect and true. How could the 'Word of God' contain contradictions? Who would be so arrogant as to delete something from the 'Word of God' or to tamper with its holiness by adding something never heard of before? That liturgical custom of ending the lessons in church with the declaration that 'This is the Word of God' is just one more part of what might be called ecclesiastical propaganda in regard to the Bible."

It is without doubt an imperfect process, but generation after generation, the Word of God contained in scripture has been communicated to persons seeking the truth by persons committed to revealing the truth. These committed revealers and seekers of truth play a vital role in keeping God's Word alive and they have a great responsibility to reveal the truth to the best of their knowledge and ability.

Few persons close to Jesus were able to read and write, and the firsthand witnesses to the ministry of Jesus and his resurrection apparently maintained no current written account. None of them spoke or wrote Greek, the original language of the Gospels, and according to all four Gospels the apostles were in hiding and no apostle was a firsthand witness to the proceedings of the last day in the life of Jesus. Instead the good news of Jesus' ministry, death and resurrection was passed on by word of mouth until it was eventually written in the Gospels starting some thirty years after his death.

The Gospels and other books and letters of the Old and New Testament were written by a variety of authors at different times and under different circumstances, and each had his own unique way of expressing the truth as he understood it. Extensive use of figures of speech seems to have been the order of the day, and this was no doubt effective considering the literacy of the time.

These authors were surely true believers of great intelligence, totally faithful to God, speaking to contemporary audiences. None of them was capable of perfectly remembering and recording what they had witnessed and been told nor did they possess any scientific knowledge. None of them understood that their writings would someday be consolidated into a "Holy Bible," undergo translation into multiple variations of most languages of the world, and be used over the next two thousand years to bring humanity closer to God.

No doubt all of the authors reached out to God for assistance and their works were influenced by His response delivered either through them or to them. In my judgment God's truth can definitely be found in the Holy Bible by seekers of truth but it is not so easily found by readers who expect the truth to pop off the page.

God's message contained in the Bible, and also in the Qur'an, is often distorted by narrow interpretation or deliberate misinterpretation of passages contained therein. All too often the narrow differences are used to distort His entire Word or the misinterpretations are used to justify actions contrary to His will. Except by influencing humanity to do it for Him, my God has no ability to stop those things from happening.

I believe there is ample reason to believe the Qur'an is being grossly misinterpreted by persons who take advantage of ambiguities in its written content and the fact that it is written in an ancient Arabic known to only a tiny minority. In this imperfect world, we should not be blind to the possibility that some who profess to reveal or seek the truth interpret the Qur'an to their personal advantage. The revelations contained in the Qur'an may well be God's revelations as Muhammad understood them and recited them to scribes, but few now understand the Arabic language used in the Qur'an. I suspect, but do not know for sure, that God's truth is in the Qur'an for those who honestly seek it. There is nonetheless much room for distortion by those who seek power rather than truth. Similar comment applies to the Holy Bible, and I fail to see how blind recitation of the writings of either book in our contemporary world brings anyone closer to God.

Both the Qur'an and the Bible are surely helpful for entering a personal relationship with *my God*, but absent intelligent reflection and personal communication with Him, I fail to see how anyone can achieve His expectations for them. Even in a world populated by imperfect people *my God's* Word continues to be revealed with ever-increasing clarity to those who are committed to a relentless search for His truth. His written word is vitally important for all of humanity in a collective sense, but He also has specific need for unique contributions from each member of humanity. The only way I know to discern that need is by direct personal communication with Him through private prayer.

Chapter Seventeen

Living Things

According to Genesis, on the Sixth Day God decided human-kind should have dominion over the fish in the sea, the birds in the sky, the livestock and everything that creeps on the earth.

The term "Sixth Day" clearly symbolizes the point in time four-teen billion years after the "First Day" when anatomically modern humans had evolved from basic life into a level of creative and intellectual superiority over all other forms of life. That point in time, only 200,000 years ago, was when I believe *my God* began to reach out to humanity.

At that same point in time *my God* also delegated humankind to have dominion over all the earth but most of those 200,000 years needed to pass before humanity began to recognize that with dominion also comes responsibility. *My God's* intention is for humanity to serve Him by creatively using all that has been created since the Big Bang, and humanity has a responsibility to ensure that by so serving Him others are not precluded from serving Him in the future.

Western civilization in particular appears obsessed with lon-gevity of life and fear of death. Longevity is often viewed as more important than life's accomplishments. All of life is precious to *my God* and all of life must be periodically renewed in order to carry out His plan for Creation. Except for humanity, no other living thing fears death, and humanity alone can comprehend that it serves as an element in *my God's* plan. Anyone who accepts His existence should understand that He epitomizes compassionate love and is incapable of acting except in love.

Those who accept *my God* have good reason to consider death as an integral part of life and not fear its finality or its process. The certainty of death is contemplated by His plan and He does not impose it on a case-by-case basis as punishment for individual actions. Life can find its own end but the circumstances and timing of death are frequently influenced by the free will endowed to all of life and continuing effects of the Big Bang, neither of which *my God* controls.

Life cut short even for the most understandable reasons or in pursuit of the noblest causes appears to require at least an accounting and often retribution. Meanwhile, denial of life for the unborn is accepted as routine and "government" has assumed the role of arbiter and enforcer of right and wrong. Fortunately, with a few exceptions, those who choose life may do so without government interference.

Human imperfection and free will are fundamental to our world and combine regularly to cause death or postpone it. Unless human death is knowingly and deliberately caused, I do not believe it is contrary to *my God's* will. When it comes to protection of human life, His will is not something to be judged by humanity; humanity is instead judged by Him.

Few have suffered a more painful or humiliating death than Jesus Christ. In my judgment, human imperfection and free will had much to do in the circumstances of Jesus' punishment and death, but many acted knowingly and deliberately. The event is far in the past and those responsible have no doubt answered to *my God* for their actions. It is not for humanity to exact punishment on those who follow them. Jesus' violent end served to dramatize his life. It continues to serve as a perfect historical example to those who follow him that Christians are instruments of an eternal God and that He does not die when Christians are killed. *My God's* eternal spirit was in and with Jesus at the end, and it exists today in all who follow the example of Jesus and invite Him in.

Some people enjoy bountiful lives while others' range from being less bountiful to downright miserable. Some would consider this *unfair*, but the gift of life is given to all of humanity, and when welcomed in, *my God* uses it to best serve Him and carry out His will. It can serve Him in a myriad of ways, and free will combined with life experiences and unique physical, intellectual and creative qualities influence how that is best done in any particular point in time and set of circumstances. Much is expected of all who invite Him in and wish to serve Him and more is surely expected from those to whom much has been provided. That said, all who would serve Him to the best of their ability are equal in the eyes of my God.

Maurice Boyd once preached that we are "dying into life" while we are "living into death," indicating that life and death as we know them are part of the same continuing process. He was fond of saying that life is a bridge meant for crossing over, not a permanent home. Maurice seemed to believe that, for those who invite God into their lives, life can be thought of as an interlude within eternity.

Chapter Eighteen

Adversity

In a physical world in need of perfecting, overcoming adversity is a necessary part of the process, and adversity in some form or other is a part of every life.

The Lord's Prayer states "Thy will be done on earth as it is in heaven." I derive from this that humanity serves *my God* best by accepting adversity as something to be overcome in transforming our world into something that mirrors His spiritual reality. *My God* needs a living presence to carry out His plan for perfecting our physical world. He no doubt knows the task is challenging and may well have selected humanity because it is the survivor of a three billion–year evolution of life in a hostile physical environment. Much adversity would appear to lie ahead in the continuing perfecting process, and humanity can best overcome it with His guidance. Rather than sheltering those faithful to Him from adversity, *my God* expects us to confront adversity in pursuit of His will, and I think He intends to be with us throughout the adventure.

Pain, suffering and humiliation are very personal forms of adversity encountered to quite varying degrees by different people. Some suffer these forms of adversity while others avoid them entirely. It would perhaps be quite a different world if *my God* could intervene directly in it, but I believe He intervenes by influencing those who turn to Him. Much pain, suffering and humiliation may be caused by persons who do not turn to God, but it often results simply from the free will endowed to all of life. Pain, suffering and humiliation are regrettably a part of many lives, but they are never *my God's* choice. He is with all who endure them, whether they believe in Him or not.

A lesson from the life and ministry of Jesus is that adversity in some form or other is a part of every life and overcoming it ultimately results in good. His ministry was all about overcoming adversity, but at its end his pain, suffering and humiliation were outside his control even though he expected them to come his way and addressed them with great dignity. The ministry of Jesus Christ transformed the world for all time, but were it not for adversity at his life's end, his actions in the face of it, and his extraordinary triumph over it, the world would probably not remember him.

Pain and suffering in particular can be personally very cruel, but *my God* is at our side for the asking, and accepting adversity as a force for good can help us find our way out. In my view, it is unrealistic to expect to avoid adversity to oneself or to those we love just because one believes in God. When we experience adversity we should know *my God* is sharing it with us. It has been very helpful to me to ask Him for the wisdom and strength needed to deal with adversity and death. Resolution of life's problems takes time, so it helps to be patient, persistent, and faithful in the knowledge that He will never desert us.

Chapter Nineteen

Good and Bad

Over almost eight decades of life I have discerned a dramatic change in attitude on good versus bad, at least in the Western world.

It may have something to do with my naïve idealism when I was a young man, but I believed then that there was such a thing as absolute good, though it may have escaped my notice that there were degrees of good and bad. I still feel that way today, but I suspect I am very much in the minority and most people think of good in relative terms.

All too often mere humans determine good and bad for others as well as themselves without *my God's* participation. Whether it is done by fiat or by majority, it would seem unrealistic for them to impose their own standards on others who disagree, but the fact that it is unrealistic doesn't stop it from happening. Many also seem inclined to define good and bad in very personal terms of what works for them in the here and now, whether it be government, business, education, personal wealth, raising children, etc. Yet what works for them may well be downright harmful to others, and, more importantly, harmful to God's intention.

We are all of us living in a world of reality and free will, and I have found it helpful to believe we are participants, with help from *my God*, in a perfecting process coordinated by Him. A process that has quite a long way to go and rarely proceeds on a straight line. For all who accept *my God* I think there exists a single standard for good and bad to guide that process. If something advances His intention for our world it is good, and if something is harmful to His intention for our world it is bad. There may be much that neither advances nor harms His intention and might be considered a gift of life itself, but we are left to determine *my God's* intention for ourselves and to discern what is good and what is bad. Fortunately, *my God* continues to communicate His intention to those who turn to Him.

I see no reason to believe good is only accomplished by those faithful to my God. Even those not faithful to Him can accomplish much good when they act in accordance with free will to advance His intention for our world. He is perfectly capable of permitting good to happen on its own without His influence.

In his letter to the Romans the apostle Paul said that God cooperates for good with all who love Him and further said, "Do not be overcome by evil but overcome evil with good." Most surely Paul's intention was for the world to understand that God also overcomes evil with good. His only intention for all who love Him and reach out to Him is that they help Him to accomplish good.

Chapter Twenty

America

"America is the only nation in the world that is founded on a creed. That creed is set forth with dogmatic and even theological lucidity in the Declaration of Independence; perhaps the only piece of practical politics that is also theoretical politics and also great literature. It enunciates that all men [and women] are equal in their claim to justice, that governments exist to give them that justice, and that their authority is for that reason just. It certainly condemns anarchism, and it does by inference condemn atheism, since it clearly names the Creator as the ultimate authority from whom these equal rights are derived." © *G.K. Chesterton (1874-1936)* What I Saw in America

To a significant extent, the American constitution embedding these endowed rights was a reaction to an English system of government under King George III that the majority living in England found perfectly acceptable. Americans today appear to accept that government of the majority should grant and deny rights even if some rights considered by our founders to be unalienable are compromised as a result. Such a government arguably has parallels to the government of King George, loved by the favored and hated by those who think their rights have been denied. What seems to be lost in the argument is the founders' principle that the only rights government is intended to protect are those endowed by God.

Unlike most civilizations, America was blessed in its formative years with extraordinary leaders, including Washington, Madison, Hamilton, Adams and Jefferson. These men were intelligent, well educated, clear-thinking, willing to sacrifice and motivated in an unselfish way to establish principles that would form the bedrock for a free civilization unlike any other in the history of the world.

Its first two centuries were also distinguished by massive immigration of persons in all walks of life who struggled to achieve the so-called American dream through their own efforts. There was surely much to criticize in how many of them accomplished it, starting with the use of enslaved persons for the first eighty years, but those combined efforts contributed in a major way to making America great in the eyes of the world. In my lifetime a culture has emerged that encourages dependency on government resources and that culture discourages many from striving to achieve. It is a controversial and complex subject far beyond the scope of this work but America in my judgment has not benefited from a culture of dependency on government.

One of the principles at the very forefront of the founding of this great country was trust in God and that principle sustained America for at least its first two hundred years as it achieved greatness in the world. Most founders were Christians and the founding documents reflected Jesus' qualities of wisdom, compassion, justice, forgiveness and restraint, but nowhere in our founding principles can one find mention of trust in Jesus Christ or even the God who revealed Himself through the life of Jesus. The First Amendment simply states that Congress shall make no law respecting an establishment of religion or prohibiting the free exercise thereof.

It was arguably the wish of America's founding fathers that participants in government take into account their individual perception of God's will as they understood it. They contemplated that some participants might deny Him, but did not contemplate that nonbelievers would someday have a disproportionate say in whether God's will is considered in the governing principles for America. Free will may permit it, but America ceases to be the nation of its founders and indeed most of its history when that happens.

Our founders left no doubt regarding their intention that the principle of trust in the truth of God should be fundamental to our public arena. They left no opening for it to be changed by a small population that believes only in itself and is not able to agree upon or even verbalize what else of a positive nature it believes. Disbelief in what others believe does not constitute belief in anything, and it is my opinion that people who believe only in themselves and cooperate with each other in order to achieve power are leading America down a slippery slope.

I think of America as an ideal that merits the very best efforts of all Americans to achieve and will probably never be totally achieved. America as an ideal has been a beacon to the world, and if most of us continue to strive for the ideal of America, this great country should continue to flourish. If we instead become a country that encourages few to cooperate toward achieving that ideal while the majority either fails to contribute or sits back in judgment we can expect less, far less.

Rather than taking sides between individuals or groups of individuals with different points of view, *my God* appears content to let participants resolve their differences on their own. He has no apparent ability to intervene with imperfect and free-willed decisions of

Americans except by influencing those who believe in Him and turn to Him. If America no longer chooses to be a nation that strives to do God's will, however imperfectly, why should America expect Him to be at its side? Nothing is inevitable except consequences.

To the extent that America permits the present to stand in the way of the ideal, or even chooses to change the principles that are fundamental to its greatness, the country risks going the way of every great civilization that preceded it. America's founders turned to the God of their belief and shared His values. I hope Americans will continue to invite Him into their lives and with His help strive for the ideal that is America.

Chapter Twenty-One

My God

My God exists as an all-knowing, eternal and infinite spiritual reality pervading all that has been, all that is, and all that will be, and He epitomizes all that is good.

It may help to comprehend His nature by personalizing Him, as I do in this work, but by using such terms as "*My God,*" "He," "Him," and "His" perhaps the enormity of that reality becomes diminished in the eyes of both believers and nonbelievers.

Humanity may well accept His enormity, but its extent is beyond comprehension. Like the air we need for physical life, His presence is invisible and will always remain so, but it is available to all who "breathe" Him into their lives. He can be perceived or "seen" in the beauty of our world and universe, the spiritual qualities of Jesus Christ and the works of humanity who have invited His guidance.

My God has been spiritually one with the Universe since the Big Bang created it from nothing fourteen billion years ago, but it is unlikely that He caused it. Far more likely in my estimation is that *my God* began after the Big Bang to work creatively with its result.

The countless components that comprise the Universe are all

very real but the arithmetic sum of everything comprising today's Universe, taking due account of what is positive and what is negative, would appear to remain virtually zero, as it was at the beginning of time. The inanimate physical Universe has been expanding and maturing on its own since the Big Bang. *My God* fully knows every detail of its evolution until the end of time but has no physical ability to influence it. He has further plans for our world and Universe, but He needs a living physical presence to accomplish it for Him and He communicates His unique requirements to all who wish to serve Him.

My God was present at the beginning of life three billion years ago in the hostile, inanimate world we now inhabit. In order for life to flourish in its environment, it was endowed from the very beginning with His free will that enabled it to survive, reproduce, and evolve on its own.

My God has no physical ability to accomplish anything in our world or Universe, but all of life has such ability to varying degrees. Anything God wishes to accomplish requires Him to influence intelligent life to cooperate with Him. Possessing the free will that all life needs to survive, humanity can choose to be either spectators or participants in life and either deniers or servants of *my God*. To cooperate with Him during physical life we need to find our way into (be reborn into) a spiritual world that co-exists with our physical world but is separate and distinct from it.

My God knows what He wants to accomplish and how and when it can best be accomplished by those who open the door to Him. He knows when He needs humanity to act and when humanity should be free to enjoy lives of their own choosing. He is fully aware that others who do not reach out to Him are pursuing their own agenda and the instruction He communicates takes that reality into account.

Intelligent life is endowed with individual free will and can choose whether to cooperate with *my God*. Before it can accept Him it needs to believe not only that He exists but also that what He asks is good. He needs spiritual leaders to help with that. If elements of intelligent life choose to deny Him, *my God* will nonetheless eventually accomplish His will without their cooperation. We err if we think God's plan can be thwarted by disbelievers or that it begins and ends with us.

My God is not a micromanager of a living earthly presence endowed with free will and instead provides guidance to those who choose to reach out to Him. While continuing effects of the Big Bang undoubtedly played a part, the course of modern history has been determined largely by intelligent life, only some of whom were influenced by Him. It is not His nature to exact earthly punishment on those who act without His guidance. Any perceived earthly punishment is the result of life's free willed activity, including one's own, and the only earthly reward within His ability to provide is the joy that comes from knowing Him and trying to serve Him.

As Jesus alluded in the prayer he taught his disciples, *my God's* will is to accomplish in our world a physical reality that mirrors His spiritual reality. His will is an ideal. In order to achieve it, He utilizes the unique and imperfect physical, intellectual and creative qualities of all who cooperate with Him, and He does it when He judges the circumstances are right.

Humility is fundamental to *my God's* nature, and He communicates His will best in response to those who accept His existence and reach out to Him. That happened for the first time thirty-eight hundred years ago with Abraham and has been happening with great regularity ever since. He has no wish to remain mysterious and He has continued to reach out to humanity in the hope and expectation that humanity would also reach out to Him and learn to know and serve Him.

Since the time of Abraham, Jews, Muslims and Christians alike have been reaching out to Him and cooperating with His will as they perceive it, always with a degree of human imperfection which *my God* forgives. His forgiveness of those who have tried and failed demonstrates the priority He places on the future. He expects those who cooperate with Him to incorporate His forgiveness into the conduct of their lives. Much more will be accomplished when that happens and He will be pleased.

Jesus reached out to *my God* and cooperated with Him, and by the invitation of his baptism, *my God* inhabited him in order to reveal His true nature and better accomplish His will. When that happened Jesus Christ took on *my God's* perfect spiritual qualities of love, wisdom, humility, justice, mercy, forgiveness, understanding, patience and free will.

The very fact that the spirit of God revealed first to Abraham and later through Jesus Christ, continues to thrive two thousand years after the humiliation and death of Jesus Christ, provides ample evidence that one cannot kill *my God* by killing those who accept Him. The world was transformed by the ministry of Jesus Christ, and ever since then, *my God's* eternal spirit has continued to inhabit all who, like Jesus Christ, welcome Him to accomplish His will through them.

When He inhabits a person *My God's* eternal spirit becomes one with his or her soul and will remain so for all of eternity. Once invited in He will not leave unless invited out, and that doesn't happen very often. Those who deny *my God* often do so because they expect Him to be their servant. Once they accept that they are His servants and that what He wants to accomplish with their assistance is good, they belong to *my God* and He belongs to them.

The act of worship is an expression of reverence and adoration that indicates a willingness to cooperate with *my God*'s will. *My God* is served best when those who worship Him also prepare themselves to best serve Him, communicate with Him personally and welcome Him into their lives. He has much to ask of those who do, but He will never expect more than what they can accomplish and His eternal spirit will be with them always.

Chapter Twenty-Two

The End of Life

I suspect, like many people, I've been concerned more with the joys and challenges of life than with the prospects of death, and my God wouldn't have it any other way. I take comfort in the Psalm 23 words of David Yea though I walk through the valley of the shadow of death I fear no evil for thou art with me.

My *God's* will is advanced each time one of us decides to uniquely serve Him, so I believe we should be concerned with how we might best do that within the time we have been given. I think He has no interest in micromanaging the lives of those who do their best to emulate the qualities of Jesus Christ and are available to Him when He needs them. We should not feel a need to apologize for joy that comes our way in the process, nor for joy that comes with simply being alive.

Thanks to the work of Stephen Hawking and others it has been easier for me to approach my end not relying on a God who is creator either of the Big Bang or life itself. I rely simply on the certainty that an infinite, all-knowing and spiritual God with only good intentions has been there from the very beginning of time. Never once since I began to really reach out to Him has He failed to respond either indirectly in a variety of ways or in the quiet of the night as I lay awake. The responses always came as enlightenment regarding what I should or should not do and they never contained anything that He intended to do without my involvement. They came on His schedule and were not always what I was hoping to receive, and I wish now that I had heeded all of them. The fact that they came at all provided me with the "preponderance of evidence" I have been seeking.

I don't think it is ever too late to call upon God, even up to death. If we call upon Him I expect Him to be with us at the end to share our pain and give us comfort. If for any reason we are unable to reach out to Him, He will also be with us if others petition on our behalf. That is His nature.

Even those with the best of intentions cause damage in the course of doing good, and the God of my belief cannot simply erase any damage resulting from bad choices we made during life. He will, after we die, continue to work for good with those who choose to cooperate with Him. That includes undoing any damage we may have left behind.

While He promises to be with us if we ask, I believe the process of our dying will be easier to bear if we recognize that there have been occasions when we have failed Him and ask for His assured redemption. We need that more than He does, and whatever bad we have done will in any event be reversed by future humanity with His guidance.

Serving *my God* to the best of our ability when we have the opportunity is all we can give Him. What more is there to give? No god that I could worship would measure us by earthly accomplishment; those accomplishments receive their own earthly rewards.

No matter when it happens, if we accept God, welcome Him to be with us, and ask for His redemption, we are His and He is ours. Dottie and I fell in love sixty three years ago and for good reason waited six years to take marriage vows that included the term "until death do us part", something not always heard at weddings today. The time is fast approaching when we will indeed be separated by death and the thought of that separation is more difficult to bear than death itself.

Mormons are offered the sacrament of Marriage for Eternity and if we knew fifty seven years ago what we know now we might have been tempted to join The Church of Jesus Christ of Latter-day Saints. It is too late for that but of one thing we are certain. The love we share is the very essence of *my God*, in this case *our eternal God*, and our love is therefore also eternal.

Rabandanath Tagore, the famous Hindu poet and philosopher, wrote that the song he came to sing remained unsung because he spent his days "stringing and unstringing" his instrument. Judging from his total works, that statement probably reflects more humility than truth, but I think Rabandanath Tagore was making a point. All of us came into this world to sing our songs together, and at the end each of us is left to decide whether or not our own song remains unsung. For all who choose to be instruments of God's will and invite Him to do His will through them, their songs will not remain unsung, and the "music" will be His.

Our Webb Institute graduating class of thirteen naval architects included my twin brother Rich and our roommate Charles Grover. Twelve of us went on to seek our fortune but Charlie entered seminary soon after graduation and continues to this day to serve God as an Episcopal priest. I thank Charlie for introducing me to Dr.

W. Norman Pittenger, a fine theologian who greatly influenced him beginning with his time at seminary, wrote about and promoted process theology, and died in 1997. Dr. Pittenger was not bothered by whether we are conscious in an afterlife or simply live on in the memory of God forever. Charlie doesn't seem bothered by it either and once told me it is God's area of competence, not his, and he trusts God to take care of it. As do I.

While I have had life I have had trials, but I also experienced great joy and I think *my God* was with me every step of the way. I chose to offer my capabilities to serve Him in my uniquely imperfect manner, and I think they were uniquely accepted by Him. I tried to discern His will, live in accordance with it however imperfectly, and seek His redemption. I believe it is never too late to reach out to Him, repent for grievous mistakes in life, and choose to be an instrument of His will.

Chapter Twenty-Three

Summing Up

It is difficult for a person of science to accept something that can't be proven. It is even more difficult to build an entire case for the meaning of life on something that will never be proven, at least in the physical world we all share. Yet that is what I have done in my life and in this work. In 1742 a distant German ancestor named Christian Goldbach developed a series of Goldbach conjectures, including one stating that any even integer greater than two can be expressed as the sum of two prime numbers. Since then many have tried but none have either proven or disproven any of his conjectures. I take comfort that I am in good company with this work and leave the reader with this to ponder:

What If science conclusively proves Stephen Hawking is correct that the Big Bang was not a singular event and God was not needed for it to happen fourteen billion years ago? What if God is thereby proven not to have created our Universe?

What If science cannot *disprove* that a purely spiritual, infinite, eternal, and all knowing God was existent at the very beginning of time itself? What if such a God does in fact exist and has full knowledge of the laws that influence everything created by the Big Bang? What if He also knows all that our Universe will be at any point in time?

What If such a God is beyond human comprehension and can only be accepted by faith? What if He exemplifies all that is good?

What If such a God is one with an infinite spiritual domain that co-exists with the finite physical Universe created by the Big Bang. What if His spiritual domain pervades our Universe?

What If, like the air we need for physical life, His presence is invisible and will always remain so, but is available to all who would "breathe" Him into their spiritual lives? What if He can be perceived or "seen" in the beauty of our world and universe, the spiritual qualities of Jesus Christ, and the works of humanity who invite Him into their lives?

What If Science proves He was not necessary for the Creation of life? What if He nevertheless has the ability to spiritually inhabit life?

What If He knew before it even existed, of a unique planet in our Universe where fundamental life in the form of organic matter would result from a chemical reaction of inorganic matter? What if He knew that planet would be uniquely hospitable to life?

What If in order for it to be sustained life needs to evolve by being periodically regenerated? What if death is fundamental to regeneration of life? What if the very life that dies during the process is vitally needed to support the new life that evolves from the process?

What If He has an eternal plan involving this unique planet, and saw in fundamental life the potential, with His help, to evolve over time into a myriad of species that could play a role in His plan? What if He considers this eternal plan to be His "Creation"? What if the myriad species includes a human species possessing minds superior to all others? What if human minds possess both the ability to communicate with Him and and having the ability to reason?

What If absent a living physical presence it is not within His spiritual power to simply make His plan for Creation happen? What if He has the ability to communicate His wishes to such a human species individually and collectively? What if He communicates through the minds of those He wishes to influence? What if humanity can *perceive* His communications rather than *hearing* them?

What If He communicates to all of humanity, and much good is accomplished when He does? What if humanity, because of free will and imperfect judgment, occasionally ignores Him and acts contrary to His will? What if the human species has the physical ability to help carry out His plan for Creation and is therefore vital to its success? What if human life is therefore precious to Him?

What If those who fail to understand such a God, expect Him to be their servant and are wrong? What if He instead would like humanity to serve Him by carrying out an eternal plan for Creation that only He understands? What if there are many ways to carry out His plan? What if He not only gives humanity flexibility in achieving it but forgives them when they fall short?

What If He knows each of us better than we know ourselves, not only our innermost thoughts and physical, intellectual, and creative capabilities but also our unique life experiences? What if He would like to call on our unique capabilities and experiences when they can best assist His plan for Creation? What if He is content to let us live our own lives when we are not needed to assist Him providing we do no harm to others or to His plan for Creation?

What If He communicates to all of humanity, and much good is accomplished when He does? What if humanity, because of free will and imperfect judgment, occasionally ignores Him and acts contrary to His will? What if He nonetheless loves them but wants them to reach out to Him and repent while they still have time?

What If He accomplishes His plan by providing guidance to those who ask for it? What if acting on His guidance requires great sacrifice? What if humanity attempts to act in accordance with His guidance and fails? What if He forgives them when they fail?

What If such a God becomes one with all who reach out to Him, sharing their pain and sorrows as well as their joys? What if it is never too late to call upon Him and repent for failure to please Him, even up to death? What if He will comfort us until the end if we ask? What if He will also comfort us if others petition on our behalf and comfort others if we ask?

What If He believes He can best accomplish His eternal plan for

Creation by inhabiting those who invite Him in? What if He only inhabits those who open the door to His existence?

What If Jesus Christ was totally inhabited by this God and epitomized His compassion, wisdom, humility, justice, mercy, forgiveness, and understanding? What if Jesus Christ is the door that one must pass through in order to be inhabited by Him? What if the door can be opened partially, fully, or not at all and humanity has the free will to decide which it will be?

What If a portion of this God's eternal spirit inhabits those who open the door to Him and becomes what is known as their "soul"? What if that soul has an eternal home in God's spiritual domain? What if God's spiritual domain is what Christians refer to as "heaven?"

What If God's infinite love is His only gift to us? What if it is all we need?

About the Author

Robert Goldbach and Dorothy, his wife of fifty-seven years, divide their time between homes in New Jersey and Nassau, Bahamas. He spent his career in the marine industry, starting as a naval architect responsible for the design and construction of fifty ocean vessels, followed by service as a corporate executive responsible for ocean and U.S. Great Lakes shipping activity for a Pittsburgh-based steel company. He is an inventor of ship technologies and was awarded seven international patents and a Certificate of Meritorious Public Service by the U.S. government. He served on many company, community and church boards and is a long-term trustee of Webb Institute, where he earned a BS in Naval Architecture and Marine Engineering. His book Faith in an Imperfect World, A Letter to My Grandchildren was published in 2009. His book Siaman's Tale, An Amazing Bahamian Adventure was published in 2013.

For more information or bookings,
log on to

www.findingmygod.net